From Death Instinct

department for
children, schools and families

Attachment Theory

From Death Instinct to Attachment Theory

THE PRIMACY OF THE CHILD
IN FREUD, KLEIN, AND HERMANN

Tomas Geyskens
and
Philippe Van Haute

Other Press
New York

Translated from the Dutch with the help of a grant from the NOW (Dutch Organisation for Scientific Research).

Production Editor: Mira S. Park

This book was set in 11 pt. Berkeley by Alpha Graphics of Pittsfield, NH.

10 9 8 7 6 5 4 3 2 1

Library of Congress Cataloging-in-Publication Data

Geyskens, Tomas.
   From death instinct to attachment theory : the primacy of the child in Freud, Klein, and Hermann / Tomas Geyskens and Philippe Van Haute.
      p. ; cm.
   Includes bibliographical references and index.
   ISBN-13: 978-1-59051-152-7
   1. Psychoanalysis. 2. Death instinct. 3. Object relations (Psychoanalysis) 4. Freud, Sigmund, 1856–1939. 5. Klein, Melanie. 6. Hermann, Imre, 1889–1984. I. Haute, Philippe van, 1957– II. Title.
   [DNLM: 1. Freud, Sigmund, 1856–1939. 2. Klein, Melanie. 3. Hermann, Imre, 1889–1984. 4. Psychoanalytic Theory. 5. Death. 6. Instinct. 7. Object Attachment. WM 460 G397f 2007]
   BF175.G483 2007
   150.19'5—dc22

2006005943

Contents

Introduction

THE DEATH INSTINCT: A SUPERFLUOUS HYPOTHESIS?

In 1920 Freud wrote *Beyond the Pleasure Principle*, in which, for the first time, he introduced the death instinct. To the present day, this concept has been in great dispute. Enthusiastically received by some (for example, Klein and Lacan) as a necessary element of metapsychology, it has been dismissed by others as a useless speculation that was clinically completely superfluous and only served to give psychoanalysis a bad name in scientific circles—the latter more pronouncedly so because Freud conceived of the death instinct as a cosmological principle at work, not only in human psychology but also in nature in its entirety. As such, *Beyond the Pleasure Principle* has all the characteristics of a meditation on the philosophy of nature, the link with clinical practice not always being so readily apparent. Regardless, it was precisely clinical problems that caused Freud to introduce this problematic concept into his theory.

Until the publication of *Beyond the Pleasure Principle*, Freud had assumed that mental life was governed by the pleasure principle.

According to this principle, all mental activity aims at attaining pleasure and at avoiding unpleasure. If, as in the case of neurosis, unpleasure does nevertheless occur, it must be traced back to a repressed infantile experience of pleasure. This means that all neurotic symptoms are the expressions of infantile sexual desires and impulses. After the First World War, however, Freud was confronted with traumatized veterans whose symptoms do not correspond to the logic of the pleasure principle. The clinical experience of war neuroses compelled Freud to reevaluate his theory of the pleasure principle. What these traumatized patients repeated again and again in their dreams and symptoms were, after all, not unconscious experiences of pleasure, but, on the contrary, painful experiences that were at no point in time pleasurable. This compulsion to repeat can also be found in the pathology of neurotic subjects and in therapy. Freud noted that during transference patients repeat not only experiences that once provided pleasure, but also infantile experiences of neglect, abuse, and humiliation that were never pleasurable. From 1920, Freud therefore felt it necessary to develop a theory of the compulsion to repeat and trauma "beyond the pleasure principle."

In *Beyond the Pleasure Principle* Freud links the compulsion to repeat to an organically rooted death instinct. The compulsion to repeat is the expression of a demonic principle at work in everyone's mental life. In this manner Freud turns the compulsion to repeat that he discovers in traumatic neurosis into the most primary dynamic principle in the psychological apparatus of all of us. By assigning it a biological basis, Freud turns the compulsion to repeat into a universal characteristic of human nature.

This generalization, from pathology to mental life as such, is characteristic for Freudian psychoanalysis.[1] Freudian psychoanalysis is indeed a *clinical anthropology*. To study the fundamental dimensions of human existence, it consults its pathological variants. Freud calls this the *crystal principle*: the subject "fractures" along lines that had

---

1. For further elaboration and justification of this claim, see Van Haute and Geyskens 2004.

previously not been visible, just like a crystal. Pathology reveals the hidden structure of normality, which must be examined from the perspective of these fault lines. In his study of human sexuality, for example, Freud (1905b) takes sexual perversions as his starting point, which he views as the exaggerations of tendencies that are present in every person. Analogously, the study of traumatic neuroses leads to the affirmation of a biologically grounded compulsion to repeat, which effectively sidelines the pleasure principle.

Does the reference to a death instinct provide a better insight into the pathological phenomena it is meant to elucidate? It is noteworthy that in the clinical texts published after *Beyond the Pleasure Principle*, Freud makes little or no mention of the death instinct. In these texts, as elsewhere, Freud is looking for an *infantile factor* that may serve to explain the pathology. Any pathology must be traced back to the experiences in early childhood that lie at its origin. In this context Freud understands traumatic neuroses as proceeding from the repetition of a vital helplessness we have all known as children. According to Freud, enduring a life-threatening situation can only cause a traumatic neurosis to come about insofar as this situation leads us into a state of complete helplessness. The confrontation with mortal danger repeats an archaic situation of helplessness. Our later anxieties are also always a repetition and the working through of this original *Hilflosigkeit*. Freud adds that this helplessness and the infantile traumas linked thereto are not contingent factors that could be avoided by, for example, a "good-enough mother" (Winnicott). Indeed, the helplessness of the child is fundamentally a helplessness with regard to its own instincts. The shortcomings of the caring adult constitute only part of the radical helplessness of the child toward its own instincts. Such primitive catastrophes are inevitable and belong in essence to everyone's childhood. Freud thus formulates a *primacy of the child*: infantile traumas are inevitable—they only differ in intensity—and they remain determinative for our later course in life. In essence the human being remains out of joint.[2]

---

2. In this context, see Van Haute 2002.

The study of traumatic neurosis confirms the existence of a universal infantile trauma at the origin of subjectivity. The "binding" and psychological working through of this trauma is consequently a universal task to which the traumatic neurosis bears witness in an exaggerated manner. According to Freud the repetition of the traumatic situation in dreams and actions is just a desperate attempt to attain an active position toward trauma in extremis. By repeating trauma we can become its subject instead of its passive victim. The affects that at the time of trauma were impossible can still be developed in its repetition. The anger, sadness, or fear that only arise in the repetition of the trauma make of the compulsion to repeat a universal academy of suffering.

What are we then to make of the death instinct? In any case, Freud's concrete discussions of pathology make it clinically redundant. The reference to infantile *Hilflosigkeit* suffices to explain traumatic neurosis and the compulsion to repeat. But from the point of view of theory, the death instinct is also superfluous. In Freud the introduction of the death instinct goes together with a redefinition of the instinct per se. From now on Freud conceives of the instinct as the urge to restore a previous state of things that the living entity has been obliged to abandon under the pressure of disturbing external forces. From the perspective of Freud's philosophy of nature, this means that inorganic nature is disturbed in its equilibrium by an external shock. The life that came to be in this way is the tendency to reestablish the original state. What is this, other than a description of the compulsion to repeat expressed in biological metaphors? What do Freud's war veterans do, other than "recreate a previous state which was lost due to disturbing external forces" (Freud 1920, p. 36)? Freud's biological theory of the death instinct turns traumatic neurosis into the model of the origin of life as such. Further, this also means that Freud's biological speculations about the death instinct refer to the infant's original *Hilflosigkeit* that he addresses in his clinical studies. In so doing, these speculations do not add anything to metapsychology but rather obscure one of its central insights: the traumatic origin of subjectivity, that is to say *the universal primacy of the child*.

We have already pointed out that from its very inception the hypothesis of the death instinct had enthusiastic adherents as well as fervent opponents. The most important and most popular defender of this hypothesis is undoubtedly Melanie Klein, who became its passionate advocate primarily from the 1930s onward. Like Freud, Klein is convinced of the need to affirm the existence of a biological death instinct in order to gain insight into certain clinical phenomena. Like Freud, she is of the opinion that these clinical phenomena teach us something about human nature as such.[3] What is also noteworthy is the following: in her clinical analyses Klein replaces the death instinct with the primacy of the *Hilflosigkeit* and that of the *infantile (vital) trauma*. Consequently reference to the death instinct is likewise redundant in the work of Klein, and can also be replaced by an affirmation of the primacy of the trauma. The death instinct is a superfluous hypothesis that adds nothing to psychoanalytic metapsychology.

THE PRIMACY OF TRAUMA:
AN UNACCEPTABLE HYPOTHESIS?

The reformulation of the theory of the death instinct in terms of a primacy of the child and in terms of a trauma that is most intimately connected to infantile helplessness does, however, have an annoying flip side. The emphasis that Freud and Klein place on infantile *Hilflosigkeit* compels them at the same time to conceive of the child's relations with its surroundings—and in particular with its mother—as a consequence of this helplessness. The child enters into a relationship with its environment because it is helpless. It loves its mother and other attending adults because it fears that without their assistance it will not survive. From this perspective the desire for contact with and attachment to the mother can only be thought of as a secondary instinct (Bowlby 1958). According to Freud and Klein, these bonds are not original tendencies and hence require deeper foundation.

---

3. In this respect, and in contrast to Freud, Klein, however, does not in the first instance refer to traumatic neurosis, but to psychosis. We shall return to this point extensively.

However, the latter is most improbable. If the urge for attachment is a secondary instinct, how can we understand children who, in spite of having been the victims of the worst abuses, appear to have an attachment to their parents and sometimes have the most unbelievable loyalty toward them? Attachment behavior, furthermore, is not a privilege proper only to humans. It also occurs among higher primates who remain dependent on their mother for a much shorter period of time. Currently we have become accustomed to understand this attachment behavior in terms of evolutionary biology and hence to underline its adaptive advantages. Why should human behavior that also occurs in animals be explained in a different fashion from what is done for animals? Attachment behavior, for example, promotes the child's protection against danger, ensures the availability of food, and makes it possible for the child to gain knowledge of the environment it grows up in via the mother (Bowlby 1969).

Therefore, it is little cause for wonder that Freud's insights into the secondary character of attachment and the relation to the object were heavily criticized from very early on. In this the so-called Hungarian school took the lead from the early 1930s. Following in Sandor Ferenczi's footsteps, Michael Balint[4] and Imre Hermann[5] forcefully resisted the idea that the infant would not, on its own and from the outset, seek out the proximity of the mother. According to Alice Balint (1937), "Most likely the earliest phase of the extra-uterine mental life . . . is directed towards objects, but this early object-relation is a passive one. Its aim is briefly

---

4. Michael Balint (1896–1970) studied medicine in Budapest, to which he returned after a short stay in Berlin where he received his analytic training. In 1938 the arrival of the Nazis forced him to emigrate to London, where he belonged to the so-called middle group of the British Society of Psycho-analysis. His main claim to fame lies in his attempts to introduce analytic concepts into medical work ("Balint groups"). His insights into "primary love" in the first months of life made him one of the forerunners of object-relations theorists.

5. Hermann (1889–1984), together with Ferenczi and Balint, is among the most prestigious representatives of the so-called Hungarian school. His work is little known, in part because the majority of his texts were not translated. He dedicated his life to the dissemination and defense of psychoanalysis in Hungary, often under difficult circumstances—National Socialism, Communism. He was one of the first to introduce ethological considerations to psychoanalytic theory.

this: 'I shall be loved and satisfied, without being under any obligation to give anything in return'" (pp. 98–99). Balint speaks of an "archaic, egotistic way of loving, originally directed exclusively towards the mother; its main characteristic is the complete lack of reality sense in regard to the interests of the love-object" (A. Balint 1939, p. 114; see also M. Balint 1952, p. 247). In the same context Hermann refers to the attachment behavior of primates, which he also identifies in humans (Hermann 1933).[6] In this way these authors resist the Freudian–Kleinian primacy of a universal trauma of which attachment behavior is supposed to be a derivative.

In particular John Bowlby has placed the problematic of attachment on the psychoanalytic agenda.[7] Although Bowlby also relied on the work of the Hungarian psychoanalysts, he primarily draws on evolutionary facts and the empirical investigations of young children. He describes a number of behaviors, such as seizing, smiling, shouting, crying, and looking, but also separation anxiety, curiosity, anger, and sadness, which according to him aim at the *proximity of the mother* (*attachment behavior*). According to Bowlby, this interest in the proximity of the mother is original and nonderivative. It is inherent in the biological nature of humans. He aims primarily to describe the normal development of situations of anxiety: from separation anxiety to fear of strangers, to the anxiety of loneliness and the real and imaginary anxieties of adulthood. According to Bowlby (1973) these anxieties can be explained from the standpoint of evolutionary theory. They are the result of natural selection and do not require a psychodynamic explanation.

---

6. This means that the Hungarian school must without a doubt be counted among the more important predecessors of the later object-relations theories. However, it would be wrong to thematize the opposition between the defendants of the primacy of trauma and those of the primacy of attachment as an opposition between orthodox Freudians and object-relations theorists. Klein, for example, defends the primacy of the death instinct and of the trauma, even though she is often considered to be the mother of object-relation theories.

7. Bowlby (1907–1990) was an analysand of Joan Rivière, but was of the opinion that Klein and her collaborators had paid too little attention to the real environment of the child. With the publication of "The Nature of the Child's Tie to His Mother" in 1958, Bowlby develops his own theory of attachment, which resulted in the famous trilogy *Attachment, Separation, and Loss*.

Bowlby believes in a normal development that may be studied as such. Pathologies only occur when this development is disturbed by external traumas. Thus he breaks with Freud's clinical anthropology and the crystal principle, which teaches that normality (psychological health) must be understood and thematized from the standpoint of pathology. At the same time, the primacy of trauma appears to be an unacceptable hypothesis. The normal development has a linear progression; in principle, the first stages can be surmounted without trace by the later stages, such that they remain without meaning or effect for the later course of life. This development is in principle disturbed only by external traumas, such as neglect and abuse.

THE PRIMACY OF TRAUMA OR THE PRIMACY OF ATTACHMENT: AN INDISSOLUBLE DILEMMA?

The work of Bowlby and his followers presents a dilemma to psychoanalysis. Either it accepts that attachment is an autonomous dimension of human existence and renounces the project of a clinical anthropology as well as the primacy of the child, or it must continue to adhere to this project (and this primacy) and enters into conflict with one of the most important theories about childhood and tendencies in contemporary empirical psychological research. Neither of these alternatives is appealing. In the first case, psychoanalysis must distance itself from its philosophical and clinical radicality and it must become merely one strain of developmental psychology among others. In the second case, it negates a dimension of human existence, the original nature of which can be doubted only with difficulty today. Is there a way out of this impasse?

To find a solution for our problem, it is useful to return to the discussion between the original protagonists of the debate with which we are concerned here.[8] We have already pointed out that the psycho-

---

8. In fact, we would also have to address Lacan's texts on the imaginary and the mirror stage. The original text about the mirror stage has been lost, but it was written in 1936 and hence dates from the same period as Klein's first significant texts and the texts of the Hungarian school to which we referred. Lacan's texts on the imagi-

analysts of the Hungarian school defend a proto-theory of attachment that anticipates Bowlby's insights into the same problematic. However, this does not mean that they also anticipate Bowlby's developmental perspective. Even though this perspective is strongly present in the work of Balint, it is missing in the work of Imre Hermann.[9] Although Hermann develops a theory of attachment *avant la lettre*, at the same time he remains loyal to the Freudian project of a clinical anthropology and to the primacy of the trauma.

Unlike Bowlby, Hermann does not rely on empirical research, but on clinical phenomena that he has encountered in his practice. In particular, he focuses on pathologies that receive little or no attention in the work of Freud: dysthymia and depressive states, erotomania, toxicomania, and dromomania (restlessness), in general pathologies characterized by a desire for either objects that are recurrently new or a desire for an old lost object.[10] As such, Hermann continues Freud's project of a clinical anthropology. Furthermore, Hermann understands attachment—or in his own words, "clinging"—as an evolutionary and primary tendency of human existence, yet adds that this tendency in human beings is complicated when considered in relation to the dynamics of cultural commandments and prohibitions. According to Hermann, the human child is prematurely separated from the mother and hence traumatic experiences belong structurally and inevitably to the world of early

---

nary are, furthermore, explicitly a discussion of Freud's theory of the death instinct (Lacan 1948) and Klein's description and thematization of the first years of life. We did not take this problematic into consideration, because it would complicate our argument needlessly. We shall deal with this problematic in a subsequent publication.

9. See, for example, Balint 1952. Balint describes how analysis is to make possible a regression to a pretraumatic object love. Once this goal has been attained the road is clear for the development of a nonneurotic "adult way of loving." This implies that the neurotic forms of object relations are the result of a contingent and not of a structural trauma. Lacan rightly comments: "For him [Balint] the child–mother relation is so fundamental that he goes as far as to say that if it is happily accomplished there cannot be any trouble except through an accident. This accident may even be the rule. This doesn't change anything. It is an accident with regard to the relation that is considered in its essential character" (Lacan 1975, p. 235).

10. In this context, Schotte [1990], following Szondi, speaks about "pathologies of contact."

childhood attachments. Initially the child can only suffer these experiences passively. Only when this separation is mediated symbolically, for example, by forbidding the attachment ("Don't hang on to your mother's apron-strings!"), may the child assume an active stance toward it. The separation becomes a cultural task and the tendency to cling becomes the object of the cultural renunciation of an instinct. The instinct to cling is torn from the merely natural evolution by the cultural prohibition. Hermann makes a strict distinction between a natural development and the subjective history that is marked by the structural traumas that have a permanent influence on our existence.

It appears that Hermann's work permits us to continue to defend Freud's project of a clinical anthropology and his insights concerning the primacy of the child without detracting from the primary character of attachment. Hermann's work is a clinical anthropology of attachment. At the same time, Hermann presents this anthropology as an alternative to the Freudian death instinct. It has as its expressed aim to cast a light on the clinical phenomena that motivated Freud to introduce the death instinct into his metapsychology. In this sense it offers a worthy alternative to Freud's original insights concerning infantile *Hilflosigkeit*, which allowed an understanding of the compulsion to repeat and aggression, but at the same time reduced attachment to a secondary instinct. Not only is the opposition between a primacy of trauma and the primacy of attachment not an indissoluble dilemma, it is indeed a false dilemma.

THE PRIMACY OF SEXUALITY:
A HYPOTHESIS OVERCOME?

One does not need to be a great specialist in psychoanalytic metapsychology in order to know that sexuality plays an important role. In his texts up until 1920, Freud presupposes that in one way or another all pathologies can be reduced to a sexual problematic. To be more precise, all pathologies are linked to a constitutive conflict between the sexual instinct and the instinct of self-preservation. What happens to this primacy of sexuality if we affirm the primacy of the child and further link that primacy with a trauma that must be situated in the sphere of attachment? Does this mean that sexuality becomes one domain among other domains in human existence and can no longer lay claim to an exceptional position in any way? Is the primacy of sexuality a hypothesis that we may drop without ado and consider overcome? Or is there still a special role reserved for sexuality in human existence?

The introduction of the concept of the death instinct in *Beyond the Pleasure Principle* relativized the importance of sexuality, the primacy of which Freud had unequivocally affirmed in his earlier writings. The reformulation of the death instinct in terms of a primacy of infantile trauma such as we find in Freud's clinical works from the same period does not in essence change this.[11]

Freud determined the helplessness of the small child from the point of view of a vital need. The child is completely dependent on the other to meet its vital needs. Consequently the constitutive trauma must be situated in the sphere of the instinct of self-preservation and not in that of sexuality. Finally, the primacy of trauma in the sphere of attachment also implies a weakening of the role of sexuality. If attachment is an original dimension in human existence, which cannot be derived from sexuality or helplessness, then it also possesses its own proper logic, which neither simply coincides with, nor can be reduced to, psychosexual development as such.

Viewed in this light, it is no surprise that the affirmation of the traumatic structure of subjectivity in Freud's later work coincides with a redefinition of the role and significance of sexuality in human existence. On the one hand, Freud conceives human sexuality more and more in the function of sexual difference and castration; on the other

---

11. The reference to an infantile trauma does not imply a return to Freud's trauma theory of neuroses from the beginning years of psychoanalysis. According to this theory, every pathology was the result of a sexual seduction by an adult. Consequently this theory was concerned with a trauma characteristic only of pathology. Trauma was not understood as an essential component of all human subjectivity (Van Haute and Geyskens 2004).

hand, sexuality according to Freud plays an essential role in the working through of the trauma.[12] Melanie Klein also understands infantile sexuality from this perspective. The oedipal problematic, which in her work appears to encompass the entire domain of infantile sexuality, allows for a working through of the primitive anxieties that are linked to the traumatic loss of the object. After all, the Oedipus complex permits understanding the absence of the object from the perspective of the rivalry with another object. The absence of the object is then no longer merely a catastrophe on which I have no grasp, but places me in the position of a rival. According to Hermann, the incest taboo and the Oedipus complex analogously transform the mother from a lost object of attachment into a forbidden object. The aggression that arises out of this experience of loss can thus be experienced as rivalry with a third party. In Freud and Klein as well as in Hermann, the sexualization of trauma makes an active stance toward it possible, so that we are no longer delivered to it as mere victims. The primacy of sexuality is therefore not a hypothesis that has been overcome but a hypothesis that needs to be reformulated.[13]

The problematic and the stakes of this book have been sufficiently determined. In the first two chapters we discuss the relationship between the death instinct and trauma in the work of Freud and Klein. We investigate likewise in which way this problematic prompted Freud and Klein to reformulate the primacy of sexuality. Subsequently we discuss the critique of the concept of trauma in Freud and Klein as leveled by the theorists of attachment, and the opposition between a psy-

---

12. For reasons that will become more apparent, both developments essentially belong together.

13. In *Confusion of Tongues: The Primacy of Sexuality in Freud, Ferenczi, and Laplanche* (Van Haute and Geyskens 2004), we examined the meaning and tenability of Freud's primacy of sexuality. We concluded that the primacy of sexuality must be replaced by the primacy of the child and of trauma and we called this primacy the shibboleth of psychoanalysis. However, this conclusion left two questions unanswered. How are we to understand the primacy of the child, and what significance can we assign to (infantile) sexuality in this perspective? The elaboration of a clinical anthropology of attachment and the reformulation of the primacy of sexuality that accompanies it allow us to formulate an answer to both of these questions.

choanalytic clinical anthropology and the classical formulation of the problem of attachment in the work of Bowlby. Finally, we inquire how both approaches can be reconciled in the work of Imre Hermann, who projects a clinical anthropology of attachment. We discuss to what extent this clinical anthropology of attachment permits us to understand the clinical phenomena that led Freud to the introduction of the concept of the death instinct and what role must be assigned to sexuality in that perspective.

1

The Death Instinct, Trauma, and Sexuality in the Work of Freud

During and after the First World War, Freud was confronted with the mental wounds that the experience of war inflicted on soldiers at the front, and on war veterans. Freud noticed especially that soldiers who had been traumatized by their experience of war repeated in their symptoms and dreams the painful experiences of which they had been the victims. This was in conflict with the pleasure principle, which Freud up until then had thought dominated the entire life of the psyche. The theory of the pleasure principle maintained that all neurotic unpleasure could be traced back to a repressed infantile experience of pleasure. This appeared an impossible task in the case of war neuroses. From 1920 onward, Freud developed a theory of the compulsion to repeat the traumas that lie "beyond the pleasure principle." We shall attempt to show that this theory reveals the traumatic structure of human subjectivity as such. In *Beyond the Pleasure Principle*, Freud (1920) places the compulsion to repeat in relation to an organically rooted death instinct. In this way Freud turns the compulsion to repeat, which he discovers in traumatic neurosis, into the most original dynamic principle in the mental apparatus of all of us. At the same time, the introduction of the death instinct threatens to obscure Freud's insights into the traumatic structure of human subjectivity, since in *Beyond the Pleasure Principle* Freud grounds the compulsion to repeat in a mythological thanatology. However, the confrontation of *Beyond the Pleasure Principle* with Freud's reflections on infantile trauma in *Inhibitions, Symptoms, and Anxiety* (Freud 1926) demonstrates how the concept of the death instinct can nevertheless become clinically relevant. Here our aim is neither to test the coherence of Freud's theory nor to fortify it. We only wish to rediscover and articulate the radical nature of Freud's thought.

Before 1920, Freud's theory was based on the primacy of sexuality and the primacy of childhood. In the final analysis, dreams, phantasies, and neurotic symptoms always find their source in sexual experiences of childhood. After 1920, Freud radically revised the place of sexuality in his theories because from then on it was no longer sexuality but trauma that was central to his theory.[1] Sexuality also had to be re-situated with regard to the traumatic core of human subjectivity and was no longer the exclusive pathogenic factor. On the contrary, its function was to modify and bind a more original trauma. To understand this re-situating of sexuality, we must elucidate the relation between the death instinct and sexuality in Freud's later work.

First, we briefly sketch Freud's theories of the pleasure principle before 1920. Then we show that Freud's early work is based on the primacy of infantile sexuality. Subsequently, we investigate how Freud's concept of the death instinct can be reinterpreted in light of the primacy of the child and how the introduction of this concept changes the role of sexuality in Freud's thinking.

PSYCHIC CONTINUITY AND THE PLEASURE PRINCIPLE

Before the introduction of the death instinct in 1920, Freud's theory was based on two intrinsically linked axioms, that of the *pleasure principle* and that of *psychic continuity*. This theory implies that the psychic apparatus is under the domination of the pleasure principle on the one hand, and that every activity of the psyche must be understood as meaningful on the other hand. Every psychic activity must be viewed as a striving for pleasure and an avoidance of unpleasure.[2] One outstanding example is Freud's concept that all dreams are wish fulfillment (Freud 1900). This statement is not the result of empirical research or

---

1. Herewith we link up to our conclusions in *Confusion of Tongues: The Primacy of Sexuality in Freud, Ferenczi, and Laplanche* (Van Haute and Geyskens 2004).

2. "In the theory of psycho-analysis we have no hesitation in assuming that the course taken by mental events is automatically regulated by the pleasure principle. We believe, that is to say, that the course of those events is invariably set in motion by an unpleasurable tension and that it takes a direction such that its final outcome coincides with a lowering of that tension—that is with the avoidance of unpleasure or a production of pleasure" (Freud 1920, p. 7).

induction but is an expression of Freud's axiom that the pleasure principle governs all psychic activity, and therefore also dreams. The rule of the pleasure principle alone, however, does not yet guarantee that all mental phenomena also have meaning and therefore can be interpreted (Freud 1900). This only becomes possible on the basis of the second axiom: that of psychic continuity.

The axiom of psychic continuity can best be illustrated by slips of the tongue or the forgetting of words. In these phenomena the *discontinuity of consciousness* comes to the fore. Before Freud, psychologists identified this discontinuity of consciousness with the discontinuity of the psyche as such. They identified the psychic with consciousness (Freud 1940a). In this psychology of consciousness, dreams, slips of the tongue, and forgetting can only be explained by a somatic factor that sometimes briefly interrupts the continuity of consciousness (Freud 1900). Of course, Freud does not deny that somatic factors can exercise influence on our mental performance. In *The Psychopathology of Everyday Life* (Freud 1901), he describes how fatigue and migraine can be conducive to the forgetting of names. But, says Freud, this does not mean that fatigue and migraine *cause* us to forget names. Somatic factors are indeed conducive to forgetfulness, but they cannot explain forgetting (Freud 1901). To elucidate the difference between conducive factors and causes, Freud uses the following analogy. When someone is robbed of his money on a dark and derelict street, at the police station he will not claim that darkness and dereliction robbed him. In this way fatigue and migraine, too, are conducive to forgetting. Yet to explain forgetting, we have to ask the question as to the mental mechanism of forgetting.

This argumentation presupposes the axiom of psychic continuity. For psychologists of consciousness, forgetting is an organically determined defect of consciousness. For Freud, in contrast, forgetting is itself an activity of the psyche. According to him the discontinuity of consciousness does not at all imply a discontinuity of the psyche. We shall illustrate this by means of an example. During a conversation with a man, a young woman is no longer able to remember the title of a book that she has read recently. Afterward, when she does remember the title, she also immediately understands why she has forgotten it beforehand. The title of the book, *Ben Hur*, in German sounds like "*bin Hure*" ["*Ich bin eine Hure*"—"I am a whore"] (Freud 1901). Therefore, the forgetting of the title of the book was determined by a chain of associations (*Ben Hur*—*bin Hure*) that had not been conscious at the time. Her erotic interest in the young man did not enter her consciousness, but did, however, cause the forgetting of *Ben Hur*. In this case it is clearly not an organic but a mental factor that brings about forgetting. The forgetting of *Ben Hur* is not a defect of memory, but is based on the influence of an unconscious chain of association. The unconscious "*bin Hure*" withdraws the similar sounding *Ben Hur* from consciousness. Freud is able to reduce forgetting to a mental mechanism, because he presupposes that behind the discontinuity of consciousness, the continuity of the psyche remains intact. The unconscious is simply this continuity of the psyche behind a discontinuous consciousness.[3] In the first instance the unconscious is then a hypothesis that allows the reduction of mysterious mental phenomena such as neurotic symptoms, dreams, and symbols, to everyday thoughts and wishes.[4]

Psychical life is characterized by continuity, and the acquisition of pleasure. We may further clarify what that means by taking a look at Freud's concept of neurotic unpleasure. If the life of the psyche is governed by pleasure, how does Freud explain the genesis of neurotic unpleasure? It does seem strange that Freud, who is confronted with the suffering of his neurotic patients on a daily basis, develops a theory in which pleasure is the ultimate end point of all mental life. In *Notes Upon a Case of Obsessional Neurosis* (*The Ratman*) (Freud 1909) we find the first indication of Freud's solution. One of Freud's patients,

---

3. For the moment we are concerned with the descriptive unconscious, and not yet the dynamic unconscious.
4. "Most of the time we forget (and this often happens to Freud himself) that the unconscious is a hypothesis. It is said to exist, it is made the effective agent of all aberrant psychical processes. And subsequently, because it exists, because it is a fact, one tries to make it speak, to know it, describe it, just as one would describe external facts. One establishes laws of its functioning, one provides it with a theory, etc. However, from a strictly epistemological point of view, all of these developments are illegitimate" (Roustang 2000, p. 65, our translation).

the Ratman, speaks about a punishment from the orient, whereby the prisoner is tied down. A pot filled with rats is attached to his posterior. The rats then make their way inside. While the Ratman tells this story his face betrays *"horror at pleasure of his own, of which he himself was unaware"* (Freud 1909, pp. 166–167, italics Freud). Freud's remarks on the Ratman's disgust fittingly illustrate how unpleasure can be understood in a theory of the pleasure principle. According to Freud, not merely the Ratman's unpleasure, but "all neurotic unpleasure is of that kind, *pleasure that cannot be felt as such*" (Freud 1920, p. 11, italics added). As a consequence of the axiom of psychic continuity and the pleasure principle, Freud can only understand neurotic unpleasure as *repressed pleasure*. We may elucidate this further by an investigation of Freud's concept of anxiety dreams in *The Interpretation of Dreams*.

On first sight anxiety dreams are a clear indication that not all dreams are wish fulfillments. Freud, however, demonstrates that anxiety dreams, too, can be traced back to "pleasure that cannot be experienced as such." In *The Interpretation of Dreams* he discusses the returning nightmare of one of his analysands.[5] As an adolescent this man repeatedly dreamed that he was being followed by a man with an ax. He attempts to escape in vain. On the level of the manifest content of the dream there can be no talk of wish fulfillment. The analysand's associations with the dream also lead to more aggressive memories. He remembers fights with his brother, which had been bloody at times, and his mother's fear that he would yet kill his brother one day. However, in this chain of associations emerges a memory of his parents. He remembers how, as a child, he had overheard his parents making love at night. This had left the impression on him of being something violent. The traces of blood that he had found in his mother's bed had reinforced his conviction. According to Freud, this series of associations explains the anxiety that accompanies the dream. The parents' intercourse had excited the child sexually, but because adult sexuality was a mystery to him, and because it concerned his

---

5. For a more extensive analysis of this dream, see Van Haute and Geyskens 2004.

parents, his own sexual excitement had scared him. Sexual excitation is transformed into anxiety.[6]

Freud understands all neurotic unpleasure as repressed pleasure. In principle, psychic representations are aimed at attaining pleasure. If these representations are not able to come into consciousness undisturbed, then pleasure cannot be experienced as such, and unpleasure results. This unpleasure is simply transformed libido. If the mental representations would get through to consciousness undisturbed, the Ratman, for example, instead of disgust, would experience a sadistic pleasure in the telling of his horrible story. This is impossible because the story of the punishment with the rats evokes in him associations with his father and his beloved, associations that are not being admitted to consciousness. Sadistic pleasure is therefore transformed into disgust. It is a pleasure that cannot be experienced as such.

The aim of analytic treatment is then to trace the psychical continuity behind the discontinuity of consciousness. This takes place via free association.[7] Through the removal of amnesia the repressed pleasure behind neurotic unpleasure can get through to conscious life. In Freud's theory of the pleasure principle the lifting of amnesia inevitably leads to the lifting of neurotic unpleasure.

INFANTILE AMNESIA AND ORGANIC REPRESSION

According to Freud, in the final analysis the therapeutic goal of psychoanalysis—to eliminate amnesia and thereby neurotic unpleasure—is nevertheless doomed to failure. The memories of our earliest childhood are, after all, radically lost. This infantile amnesia is in essence linked to what Freud calls "organic repression." This repression

---

6. "I have explained this anxiety by arguing that what we are dealing with is a sexual excitation with which their understanding is unable to cope and which they also, no doubt, repudiate because their parents are involved in it, *and which is therefore transformed into anxiety*" (Freud 1900, p. 585, italics added).

7. This is a method that consists of the speaking out of all thoughts and ideas that occur to us without distinction. The method is the basis of psychoanalytic technique. With this technique unconscious connections can be brought to light.

of the infantile experiences of pleasure, in particular anal pleasure, lies at the origin of specifically human affects of shame and revulsion, and of the typically human interest in cleanliness and order.

Consequently Freud considers the moral affects of human beings according to the model of neurotic unpleasure. Just as neurotic unpleasure refers to a core of infantile pleasure that can no longer be regained, affects of disgust and shame are based on an organic repression of primarily anal experiences of pleasure in infancy. The reference to something organic or biological implies that organic repression is universally a human, necessary, and insurmountable process that is not rooted in nurture and cannot be undone.[8] According to Freud, the oral and anal experiences of pleasure of infancy later become sources of unpleasure, disgust, and shame, because in the development of the child the visual comes to dominate the other senses more and more.[9] According to Freud (1930), this goes together with the loss of the erogenous significance of smell and taste, and with the genesis of a revulsion from the excremental.

When at the budding of adult genital sexuality during puberty the memory traces of these infantile experiences of pleasure are cathected anew, they evoke disgust or shame instead of pleasure.[10] That which Freud calls infantile sexuality retroactively (*nachträglich*) becomes the prototype of that which is disgusting and which we do not talk about.

The experiences of pleasure of our childhood are thus radically lost. They cannot be remembered consciously and when they are cathected again later, they evoke unpleasure instead of pleasure. Infantile amnesia and organic repression are two aspects of the same phenomenon: the child

---

8. And yet here, too, we are not dealing with a somatic defect. As with forgetting in general, Freud rather understands infantile amnesia as a (biologically founded) psychological process that lies at the origin of typically human affects such as shame and disgust.

9. In the following chapter we shall return in depth to the importance of the visual and its relation to the primal repressed.

10. For a more elaborate discussion of infantile amnesia and organic repression, see Geyskens 2001 and Van Haute and Geyskens 2004.

in us is radically lost to consciousness[11] and later infantile pleasure only shows itself in disgust, shame, and unpleasure.

The organic repression of infantile sexuality makes neurosis invincible. After all, it implies that infantile amnesia and the unpleasure that refers to our infantile experiences of pleasure are not specific to neurosis as such. On the contrary, they are universal human experiences. In this way Freud transforms his theory on neuroses into a clinical anthropology.[12] Free association (that is to lead to making psychic content conscious) inevitably runs up against infantile amnesia. The lifting of neurotic unpleasure must of course clash with the organic repression that has transformed infantile pleasure into unpleasure. Through this emphasis on the unbridgeable gap between adulthood and infancy, Freud places amnesia and unpleasure, and hence neurosis, at the heart of human subjectivity.[13]

TRAUMA AND THE COMPULSION TO REPEAT

The confrontation with a number of new clinical phenomena forced Freud at the beginning of the 1920s to abandon these insights and to drastically reorient his thinking. The study of war neuroses taught Freud that the pleasure principle and psychic continuity are not originally given, but must be acquired. This insight went hand in hand with the introduction of a new theory of instincts with the death instinct at its center. First we discuss how Freud arrives at the introduction of the death instinct from an analysis of war neuroses in *Beyond the Pleasure Principle* (Freud 1920). Then we demonstrate how this idea of a death instinct, or instinct of self-destruction, obscures rather than elucidates

---

11. Consequently infantile amnesia makes total transparency of consciousness impossible

12. See Van Haute and Geyskens 2004.

13. Any medical or sociopolitical "solution" for neurosis or the discontents of culture is therefore inevitably on the road to *Seelenmord* (soul murder) because it denies the connection with our lost childhood.

how, from 1920 onward, Freud begins to develop a theory of the traumatic origin of human subjectivity.

During and after the First World War, Freud was confronted with a new clinical phenomenon. Soldiers returning from the frontline showed all sorts of bizarre neurotic symptoms. They could not move without shaking terribly, and they took fright at the least sound. During their sleep they had horrific nightmares in which they relived their most horrible war experiences. During the day, however, they were not concerned with these traumatic memories. On the contrary, they did their best not to think of them. Freud had a special interest in these nightmares because they appeared to forcefully contradict his conception of dreams as wish fulfillment. Traumatic dreams cannot be considered imaginary wish fulfillment. They repeat a traumatic experience that never could have evoked pleasure. Neither can its repetition be motivated by the pleasure principle. The compulsion to repeat that characterizes those dreams indicates that the mental apparatus cannot exclusively be thought to function as a "pleasure machine." In *Beyond the Pleasure Principle*, Freud (1920) states that the function of the compulsion to repeat instead consists of the development of anxiety. How are we to understand this?

Traumatic experiences are often characterized by violence, but equally by their sudden and unexpected character. Traumatic force increases if one is confronted with it unprepared and without anxiety. Anxiety is already a form of preparation, even if you do not yet quite know what to expect.[14] In traumatic situations the psychical apparatus is in no condition to develop any anxiety, however. Trauma comes unexpectedly or is too overwhelming for me to react to it, even with anxiety.[15] Only after trauma can I react with posttraumatic anxiety,

---

14. "Anxiety describes a particular state of expecting the danger or preparing for it, even though it may be an unknown one" (Freud 1920, p. 12).

15. "In the case of quite a number of traumas the difference between systems that are unprepared and systems that are well prepared through being hypercathected may be a decisive factor in the outcome: though where the strength of a trauma exceeds a certain limit, this factor will no doubt cease to carry weight" (Freud 1920, p. 32).

recurrent nightmares and so on. These posttraumatic anxiety dreams indicate that dreams may have another function than wish fulfillment. The anxiety that during trauma was impossible must be developed afterward. Anxiety is, as it were, the energy that is necessary to "bind" trauma after all. This posttraumatic anxiety cannot be conceived of as a pleasure that could not be experienced as such. Freud's earlier theory of anxiety as (un)pleasure or repressed pleasure is shipwrecked on posttraumatic anxiety. The sole rule of the pleasure principle is broken.[16] The repetition or reliving of traumatic situations is motivated not by pleasure, but by the need to master trauma psychologically.

Relinquishing the sole rule of the pleasure principle has a vast impact on the course of analytic treatment. Freud wrote an article in 1914 in which he dealt with the compulsion to repeat: "Remembering, Repeating, and Working Through" (Freud 1914a). In that article Freud describes repetition in analysis as resistance to memory. Instead of remembering the repressed, the analysand repeats that which he cannot remember. He acts it out.[17] Freud gives the example of an analysand who stubbornly resists the interpretations of the analyst. According to Freud this stubbornness is a repetition of the stubbornness displayed by the analysand toward his father as a child. The analysand cannot remember his earlier attitude toward his father and hence repeats it in his relation with the analyst.[18] In this manner the compulsion to repeat maintains the repression (Freud 1914a).

In *Beyond the Pleasure Principle*, however, Freud discovers that what is repeated in the analytic situation sometimes are experiences from childhood that can never have been pleasurable. He writes, "But we now come to a new and remarkable fact, namely that the compulsion to repeat also

---

16. "These dreams are endeavoring to master the stimulus retrospectively by developing the anxiety whose omission was the cause of the traumatic neurosis. They thus afford us a view of the function of the mental apparatus which, though it does not contradict the pleasure principle, is nevertheless independent of it and seems to be more primitive than the purpose of gaining pleasure and avoiding unpleasure" (Freud 1920, p. 32).

17. "He does not reproduce it as memory but in deed, he *repeats* it, in truth without any awareness that he repeats it" (Freud 1914a, p. 136, italics Freud).

18. See Van Haute and Geyskens 2002.

recalls from the past experiences which include no possibility of pleasure, and which can never, even long ago, have brought satisfaction *even to instinctual impulses which have since been repressed*" (Freud 1920, p. 20, italics added). Freud came to the conclusion that infantile experiences of neglect, abuse, or humiliation were also being repeated and relived in the relation to the analyst. Also in the analytical situation Freud encounters a traumatic core that cannot be understood on the basis of the pleasure principle. Trauma repeats itself, even though this repetition cannot be motivated by any pleasure. The unpleasure that accompanies trauma cannot be considered repressed pleasure, as it is in the case of the Ratman.

This also means that in analysis the compulsion to repeat can hardly be understood as resistance to memory. Would it not be less painful to remember (infantile) traumas or to express them in dreams, rather than to repeat them and to relive them as a current experience (Freud 1920)? In *Two Types of War Neurosis*, Freud's colleague and friend Sandor Ferenczi (1916) writes: "Many people behave similarly who were victims of sexual assaults in their childhood. Later they have the compulsion to expose themselves anew to similar experiences as though they were trying to control the originally unconscious and uncomprehended experience by a subsequent conscious one" (p. 143). Ferenczi's remark suggests that the compulsion to repeat is motivated by an attempt to repeat the trauma after the fact, in order to experience it for the first time consciously. When we speak of a *traumatic experience*, this is a contradiction in terms. Trauma makes a direct experience in the proper sense of the term impossible. It deactivates psychical activity as such. The repetition during the course of the analytic cure is then not so much resistance, but rather the ultimate attempt to reintegrate trauma into the world of experience of the subject. *Acting out* is not resistance to memory, but an attempt at repair, an attempt to "subjectivize" traumatic events before being able to represent them in dreams or memories. The infantile experience of being abandoned, for example by the parents, therefore will first be reexperienced in the relation to the analyst, before this experience can constitute the material for dreams and memories.[19]

---

19. See McDougall 1996.

These experiences clearly demonstrate that the compulsion to repeat cannot be understood from the perspective of the pleasure principle. The repetition is not motivated by the attainment of pleasure or by the avoidance of unpleasure.

War neuroses and infantile traumas that are being repeated during treatment are not the only phenomena that point to a "beyond the pleasure principle." Freud also analyzes the innocent play of his grandson. This toddler had come into the habit of throwing away from himself all the things that he could lay his hands on. He accompanied every throw with the cry of "o-o-o-o," which according to Freud meant "*fort*" (gone). Freud analyzes this game as follows: The one-and-a-half year old was a "good boy" who was very attached to his mother. He was very obedient and "certainly not precocious in his intellectual development." Freud adds that "he never cried when his mother left him for a few hours" (Freud 1920, p. 14). This does not mean, however, that he was indifferent to his mother's absence. Initially the child suffered the loss of his mother passively. This passivity implies that the child is not able to react to the loss of the mother with anger, sadness, or anxiety. The loss is too overwhelming. The throwing away of all sorts of objects is a repetition of this situation. This repetition cannot be motivated by pleasure. The loss of the mother was not at all a source of pleasure, and neither can its repetition result in the gain of pleasure. Neither is the repetition of the traumatic situation merely the return of the trauma. By repeating the trauma the child assumes an active position toward it. During the repetition it becomes the subject of the trauma rather than its passive victim. In this manner, affects that at the time of the trauma were impossible may afterward be developed after all. The anger, sadness, or anxiety that only becomes possible in the repetition of the trauma, turns the compulsion to repeat into a school of suffering (Ferenczi 1934). Only once the child has learned to suffer in repetition, can it also experience pleasure in the repetition of the trauma. In this way the throwing away of objects may receive the meaning of revenge upon his mother, and so on. In this way the compulsion to repeat may be subsumed under the government of the pleasure principle.[20] The compulsion to repeat in traumatic neuro-

---

20. We will return to this point later on in this chapter.

ses, in transference, and in the life of the child shows that the pleasure principle does not have the last word in the mental life of the human being. The first task of the compulsion to repeat consists in acquiring an active position toward a more original state of radical passivity and helplessness. This task is not an expression of the pleasure principle but it precedes the pleasure principle.[21]

The unpleasure of trauma cannot be understood from the perspective of Freud's earlier theory of unpleasure as pleasure that cannot be felt as such. After all, here unpleasure is not so much the result of a discontinuity in consciousness but rather the result of a hole or wound in psychic life itself (*Loch im Psychischen*).[22] In the case of a trauma, unpleasure is not caused by an earlier experience of pleasure not being able to get through to consciousness. The compulsion to repeat evokes an unpleasure that can never have been pleasure. The forgetting of trauma is not the result of repression.[23] It is the result of the impossibility of reacting to trauma with either attention or anxiety (Freud 1920). This only becomes possible retrospectively via the detour of the compulsion to repeat.

A DEATH INSTINCT?

According to Freud, the compulsion to repeat makes a demonic impression (Freud 1920). We first highlight two examples in which this demonic character becomes evident. In *Beyond the Pleasure Principle*, Freud (1920) gives the example of a woman who married three times,

---

21. "But it is impossible to classify as wish fulfillments the dreams we have been discussing which occur in traumatic neuroses, or the dreams during psycho-analysis which bring to memory the psychical traumas of childhood" (Freud 1920, p. 32).

22. "We describe as traumatic any excitations from the outside which are powerful enough to break through the protective shield. It seems to me that the concept of trauma necessarily implies a connection of this kind with a breach in an otherwise efficacious barrier against stimuli" (Freud 1920, p. 29).

23. In Freud's theory only representations that have in any case once been pleasurable can be subject to repression in the strict sense of the term. Such "futilities," however, are willingly being overlooked in contemporary psychoanalytic discussions.

each time with a man who shortly after the marriage became ill. Three times the woman has to take care of the husband on his deathbed. Here the repetition indeed gives the impression of something fateful or demonic. Another example in which the demonic character of the compulsion to repeat comes to the fore we shall borrow from the film *The Deer Hunter*. An American soldier in Vietnam who has been captured by the Viet Cong is witness to a gruesome game of Russian roulette. His fellow inmates either scream or attempt to calm each other. He himself does not react. At first sight he is the one who was able to remain composed in the traumatic situation. But later, back from the front, he himself begins to play Russian roulette in a compulsive fashion. During one of those games he shoots himself in the head. By actively repeating the trauma to which he had been submitted without reacting, he attempts to overcome it. The anxiety and panic that did not come to full development during the trauma must be evoked retroactively.[24] This compulsion to repeat, which makes a demonic impression when it goes against the pleasure principle, is not only at work in traumatic neurosis but, according to Freud, also in the analytic cure and in the mental life of the child (Freud 1920).

Freud (1920) asks the question of how this compulsion to repeat is linked with "the predicate of being instinctual" (*dem Triebhaften*)— a question that appears to be the result of a confusion of tongues. It is correct that the compulsion to repeat makes an instinctual (*Triebhaft*) impression. "Instinctual" then means that the subject is delivered into the hands of the compulsion to repeat and appears to be bewitched by an unmotivated compulsion. Instinctual here more or less means demonic. However, in *Beyond the Pleasure Principle* Freud conceives of this instinctual aspect in terms of a biological instinct as well, like the sexual instinct or the instinct of self-preservation. For Freud the compulsion to repeat is the expression

---

24. "At the same time the pleasure principle is for the moment put out of action. There is no longer any possibility of preventing the mental apparatus from being flooded with large amounts of stimulus and another problem arises instead—the problem of mastering the amounts of stimulus which have broken in and of binding them in the psychical sense so that they can then be disposed of" (Freud 1920, pp. 29–30).

of a biologically rooted instinct to self-destruction, which is said to show itself in the general tendency of living beings to return to an inorganic state.

In this fashion Freud severs the links to the evolutionary biology on which his preceding theory was based. When Freud speaks about the sexual instinct or about the instinct of self-preservation, he explicitly refers to Darwinian biology (Freud 1915a). But when he posits that the compulsion to repeat gives the impression of being instinctual, the reference to evolutionary biology is missing. In truth, from the perspective of Darwinian biology, seeking to explain evolution on the basis of the selection of characteristics that constitute an adaptive advantage, a death instinct is pure nonsense. The instinct to self-destruction can hardly provide any adaptive advantage. In *Beyond the Pleasure Principle*, Freud consequently projects his very own philosophy of nature in which he introduces an entirely new concept of the instinct. He writes: "It seems then that an instinct is an urge inherent in organic life to restore an earlier state of things which the living entity had been obliged to abandon under the pressure of external disturbing forces" (Freud 1920, p. 36). It is not difficult to see that Freud's new definition of the instinct is simply a description of the compulsion to repeat, formulated in biological metaphors. Indeed, war veterans repeat their traumas so as to "restore an earlier state of things which they had been obliged to abandon under the pressure of external disturbing forces" (Freud 1920, p. 36). Freud's biological theory of the death instinct turns traumatic neurosis into the model of the genesis of life as such. According to Freud, lifeless matter was brought off-balance by an original trauma. Life is the tendency of the inanimate to restore this equilibrium.[25] In this manner Freud can claim that the most fundamental striving of life aims for its own dissolution. Life is a diversion on the way to death, just as the repetition of trauma is

---

25. "The attributes of life were at some time evoked in inanimate matter by the action of a force of whose nature we can form no conception. It may perhaps have been a process similar in type to that which later caused the development of consciousness in a particular stratum of living matter. The tension that arose in the previously inanimate matter, strives towards its own dissolution, the first instinct had become a reality, the instinct to return to the inanimate" (Freud 1920, p. 38).

an attempt to overcome that trauma. Freud's fable about the genesis of life turns into an attempt to understand the process of becoming according to the model of the compulsion to repeat. As a metaphysical conception of becoming, Freud's perspective is an unconvincing alternative to Nietzsche's will to power or Schopenhauer's will. From the clinical perspective, on the other hand, this death instinct is a superfluous biologizing of the compulsion to repeat. Freud appears to understand this when he claims that the death instinct might be a philosophical phantasy created to help "bear the burden of existence" (*um die Schwere des Daseins zu ertragen*).[26]

Whatever the case may be, in *Beyond the Pleasure Principle* Freud develops a theory that turns the compulsion to repeat into a universal characteristic of the mental life of all of us. The compulsion to repeat is not particular to traumatic neurosis but is part of the life of the psyche as such. *Beyond the Pleasure Principle*, then, becomes a good example of Freud's intention to study what is normal from the perspective of pathology. In traumatic neurosis the compulsion to repeat that governs the life of us all is revealed and magnified. To understand this, we must return to Freud's analysis of traumatic neurosis. In *Inhibitions, Symptoms, and Anxiety*, Freud (1926) returns to the problem of traumatic neurosis, and also deals with the inevitable traumas of childhood.

THE REPETITION OF PRIMITIVE CATASTROPHES

In *Inhibitions, Symptoms, and Anxiety*, Freud (1926) investigates the etiology of traumatic neurosis. At first sight it seems self-evident how a traumatic neurosis comes to be. It is caused by the confrontation with a life-threatening situation. The war neurosis or accident-neurosis follows a situation of fear of death. But according to Freud, fear of

---

26. "It may be, however, that this belief in the internal necessity of dying is only another of those illusions which we have created *um die Schwere des Daseins zu ertragen* [to bear the burden of existence]" (Freud 1920, p. 45).

death as such cannot cause a neurosis. We have no representation of death. According to Freud, this means that fear of death does not really play a part in the etiology of neurosis. This argument is not very convincing. Is it not precisely the fact that we cannot imagine death, which heightens its fearful character? Freud does not pursue this issue further.[27] Another aspect of his doctrine of neuroses is more important to understand—his concept of traumatic neurosis: neurosis can only come about through the intervention of an infantile factor.[28]

The experience of the life-threatening situation only leads to a traumatic neurosis, according to Freud, because it brings us into a situation of utter helplessness. In contrast to death, which none of us has experienced, all of us have lived through such situations of total helplessness. When a small child is left alone, he or she will in the first instance cathect the memory trace of its mother. However, this hallucinatory wish fulfillment quickly gives way to desperation. Without the mother, the child is, after all, completely helpless in the face of its own instincts. The vital needs of hunger and thirst, in particular, cannot be allayed without the care of an adult. These instincts that assault the child from within burden it with an unpleasure that it cannot get rid of, and in the face of which it is utterly powerless (Freud 1926). The child is inundated by a pain that is literally unimaginable.[29] Such primitive catastrophes cause posttraumatic stress. The child becomes anxious and attentive. It starts to be on guard for signals that announce the repetition of such a psychic catastrophe. In this manner the child learns to understand the absence of the mother as a danger as such. The child now anticipates the state of unpleasure and desperation that may come about

---

27. In this context, see Van Coillie 1998, 1999.

28. "In view of all that we know about the structure of the comparatively simple neuroses of everyday life, it would seem highly improbable that a neurosis could come into being merely because of the objective presence of danger, without any participation of the deeper levels of the mental apparatus" (Freud 1926, p. 129).

29. "The infant who started with a fear he was dying, ends up by containing a nameless dread" (Bion 1962, p. 96).

through the absence of the mother. The loss of the mother hence becomes a signal of this situation of helplessness.[30]

This reference to archaic situations of anxiety of the baby clarifies the infantile factor in traumatic neurosis. It is not the danger to life as such that is traumatic, but rather the situation of radical passivity and helplessness that we have all experienced as children. The confrontation with a threat to our life repeats this archaic situation of helplessness.[31] In this way Freud identifies an infantile factor that lies at the basis of traumatic neurosis. Our later anxieties, too, are always a repetition and continued effect of this original *Hilflosigkeit*.

It has to be remarked that infantile traumas are never exclusively the effect of the psychological and pedagogical qualities or shortcomings of the mother. The helplessness of the child is ultimately helplessness in the face of its own instincts. The shortcomings of the caregiver are merely reflections of this radical helplessness of every child toward its own instincts. This means that primitive catastrophes are inevitable and essentially part of everyone's childhood. For someone like Winnicott, who placed a great emphasis on the influence of infantile trauma, but for whom the death instinct was not an important concept, these infantile traumas are accidental and therefore can be avoided by a "good-enough mother." He writes: "There are roughly speaking two kinds of human being, those who do not carry with them a significant experience of mental breakdown in earliest infancy and those who do carry around with them such an experience and who must therefore flee from it, flirt with it, fear it, and to some extent be always preoccupied with the threat of it" (Winnicott 1989, p. 122). For Freud, on the other hand, there is only one kind of human being. All of us have lived through the archaic traumas that are inevitably connected

---

30. "It is the absence of the mother that is now the danger; and as soon as that danger arises the infant gives the signal of anxiety, before the dreaded economic situation has set in" (Freud 1926, p. 138). According to Freud, the attachment to the mother is based on the fear of the child that its needs will remain unsatisfied. For a critique of this view, see Chapter 3, this volume.

31. Kamikaze pilots did not scream the name of their emperor, but for their mothers.

to the helplessness of our early childhood. In truth, not all of us are traumatized equally, but this distinction in severity can only be gradual for Freud.

By linking traumatic neurosis with an original infantile trauma, Freud generalizes the compulsion to repeat as a universal human phenomenon. In *Inhibitions, Symptoms, and Anxiety*, Freud has no need of a reference to a mythological biology for this generalization. The compulsion to repeat infantile traumas shows itself not only in traumatic neurosis, but also in transference, and more generally in our need to be loved. The helplessness of babies is a universal human phenomenon, and "[this] biological factor, then, establishes the earliest situations of danger and creates the need to be loved which will accompany the child through the rest of its life" (Freud 1926, p. 155).[32] In the infantile factor that lies at the basis of traumatic neurosis, Freud discovers a universal experience of radical *Hilflosigkeit*.[33] Freud's theory of the death instinct, therefore, may be analyzed as a theory of the traumatic core of the unconscious.[34] The most original psychic dynamics consists of fleeing this infantile traumatic core, to flirt with it, and to always have to be on guard against its possible return in the compulsion to repeat. Freud here affirms a primacy of the child, which replaces the primacy of sexuality.

Freud's theory of the death instinct is the affirmation in disguise of the primacy of a vital trauma that forces him to redefine the place of

---

32. This means that Freud can only understand the problem of attachment as a secondary instinct. Attachment is an effect of the biological helplessness of the child. The child seeks the proximity of the mother because it needs her to satisfy its vital needs. We shall return to this point extensively in Chapter 3.

33. In *Inhibitions, Symptoms, and Anxiety*, Freud bases love on the helplessness of the child. Before the introduction of the death instinct Freud conceived of sexual libido as the origin of love (Van Haute and Geyskens 2004). Evidently this change has important consequences for the concept of transference-love in the psychoanalytic cure. We are unable to elaborate this further here.

34. "At any rate, the earliest outbreaks of anxiety, which are of a very intense kind, occur before the super-ego has been differentiated. It is highly probable that the precipitating causes of primal repression are quantitative factors, such as an excessive degree of excitation and the breaking of the protective shield against stimuli" (Freud 1926, p. 94).

sexuality in his theory. The analysis of masochism and fetishism in his later texts enables Freud to rethink his theory of sexuality. In this resituating of sexuality too, the traumatic experiences of childhood play an important role. Freud describes the prohibition of anal erotism[35] and the confrontation with sexual difference as the most important modifications of the primitive catastrophes of the infant as we have described them above. In Freud's later work, sexuality primarily receives the function of "binding" an original trauma. We first discuss masochism and its relation to anal eroticism, and afterward castration and the denial of sexual difference.

THE FIRST TABOO

In *Jokes and Their Relation to the Unconscious*, Freud (1905a) posits plainly what, according to psychoanalysis, belongs to the domain of sexuality: "The sexual material . . . includes more than what is peculiar to each sex; it also includes what is common to both sexes and to which the feeling of shame extends—that is to say what is excremental in the most comprehensive sense" (p. 97).[36] Before 1920, Freud addressed the issue of anal eroticism in several of his texts.[37] But in his later texts the reference to anal pleasure has largely disappeared. At the same time he pays more and more attention to aggression, masochism, and guilt in his later work. Before 1920 he always linked these topics to anal erotism. Is it then not the case that anal erotism in Freud's later work is absent because it is (implicitly) omnipresent?

---

35. It is important not to lose sight of the fact that for Freud the terms *erotic* and *sexual* are interchangeable; on this point see Van Haute and Geyskens 2004.

36. Freud pursues this issue more extensively in his preface to the German translation of J. G. Bourke's *Scatologic Rites of All Nations* (Freud 1913b).

37. In this connection see: *Three Essays on the Theory of Sexuality* (Freud 1905b), *Jokes and Their Relation to the Unconscious* (Freud 1905a), *Character and Anal Erotism* (Freud 1908a), *Notes Upon a Case of Obsessional Neurosis* [The Ratman] (Freud 1909), *The Disposition to Obsessional Neurosis* (Freud 1913a), *On the Transformation of Instincts, as Exemplified in Anal Erotism* (Freud 1917a), and *A Child Is Being Beaten* (Freud 1919).

We will attempt to argue the point by a reading of Freud's most important text on the relation between the death instinct and sexuality, *The Economic Problem of Masochism* (1924), in which Freud asks how we can derive pleasure from unpleasure. That we do that is beyond dispute. The clearest illustration is perverse masochism. But we also call people who carry the burden of an excessively strict conscience "masochists" even though they clearly do not experience any genital pleasure from their self-inflicted torture.[38] Perverse as well as moral masochism, according to Freud, is based on *erogenous masochism*. Freud describes this erogenous masochism as an erotization of the death instinct, but his description remains very abstract. We paraphrase it as follows: The organism evacuates the death instinct, which in the first instance aims toward self-destruction, to the outside. The aggression toward objects in the outside world is then a secondary phenomenon. Aggression is self-destruction shifted onto the outside world. But, says Freud, this never fully succeeds. Part of the death instinct remains aimed at the organism itself. The only way to deal with this tendency to self-destruction is to gain pleasure from it (Freud 1924). The death instinct is erotized.

We have referred to the death instinct as a superfluous biologization of the compulsion to repeat infantile traumas. How then can we understand the erogenous masochism that Freud describes in 1924 as an erogenization of the death instinct? Freud primarily postulates this erogenous masochism in order to explain moral masochism. Yet in *The Economic Problem of Masochism* he also suggests a less abstract origin of moral masochism. The sense of guilt and moral conscience emerge, according to Freud, due to the cultural suppression of the instinct. "The first instinctual renunciation is enforced by external powers, and it is only this which creates the ethical sense which expresses itself in conscience and demands a further renunciation of instinct" (Freud 1924, p. 170).

---

38. "Yet there must be some meaning to the fact that linguistic usage has not given up the connection between the norm of behavior and erotism and calls these self-injurers masochists too" (Freud 1924, p. 165).

What are we to make of this "first instinctual renunciation" and how can the frustration of an instinct as such cause the genesis of conscience? It is evident that frustrations such as the primitive catastrophes we described in the foregoing do not lead to the genesis of conscience. In *On Narcissism, An Introduction* (1914b) and in *Three Essays on the Theory of Sexuality* (1905b), Freud had already subjected the genesis of conscience to investigation. Maybe these texts can help us to understand the moral masochism and also to get insight into the nature of the erogenous masochism that, according to Freud, forms its basis.

In *On Narcissism, An Introduction*, Freud (1914b) argues that conscience is the heir to the voice of the parents. This external origin of conscience comes to light in paranoia. The paranoiac hears voices that exclusively address him in an imperative or prohibitive tone. The voices always have a hostile tone.[39] From this analysis it seems clear that the "external force" that causes the first distance to the instinct and hence the genesis of morality is the voice of the parents. Not just any frustration, but a prohibition pronounced by the parents is the origin of conscience. In *Three Essays on the Theory of Sexuality*, Freud is more precise about this conception of the genesis of conscience: "The history of the first prohibition which a child comes across—*the prohibition of getting pleasure from anal activity and its products*—has a decisive effect on the whole development" (Freud 1905b, p. 187, italics added). The origin of conscience is a parental prohibition, and the first prohibition concerns anal erotism. What then is so special about the prohibition of anal pleasure? What makes this prohibition into the prototype of all later prohibitions and taboos?

At a certain stage of its development the child is inevitably confronted with one or another form of toilet-training. This is the first step in the "cultural suppression of the instincts" (Freud 1924, p. 170). For the first time the child has to discover that there appears to be a break between what is good and what is pleasurable. Nothing in children's

---

39. "His conscience then confronts him in a regressive form as a hostile influence from without" (Freud 1914b, p. 96).

instinctual life prepared them for this.[40] After the primitive catastrophe of the baby that in the absence of the mother is given over to its own instincts, the child is now subjected to these new and mysterious whims of adults. However, this time the child is not passively and helplessly subjected to an all-powerful other. Ultimately the child will have to obey to the demands of toilet-training, albeit only so as not to lose the love of the adult on which he or she is so dependent for self-preservation. However, there remains a margin of stubbornness, deferment, and obstinacy (Freud 1908a). According to Freud, the child regards the contents of its bowels as "the first gift" the little creature can give; "by producing them he can express his active compliance with his environment and, by withholding them, his disobedience" (Freud 1905b, p. 117). The positions we assume toward this first prohibition as a child determine our later attitude toward authority, fate, and death. Ultimately we comply, but in the meantime there is time for deferment, rebelliousness, and stubbornness, and not merely for desperation and helplessness. In this case the activities of the child are not threatened to the same extent as in the case of the archaic traumas of hunger and thirst. Pleasure rather than survival is threatened.[41]

Let us return to *The Economic Problem of Masochism* (Freud 1924). Moral masochists are people who, during their analytic cure as well as in their life, continually appear to be looking for punishment by a parental power. Even though they are not being tortured by conscious feelings of guilt, their actions appear to be motivated by an unconscious need for punishment (Freud 1924). In this context Freud refers to Russian character types that seem to be pursued by destiny: "In order to provoke punishment from this last representative of parents [des-

---

40. Freud nevertheless maintained the idea of an organic repression of anal pleasure. This entails that even without any nurture anal pleasure is transformed into disgust. Yet this organic repression does not remove the traumatic impact of the prohibition.

41. In *Civilization and Its Discontents*, Freud returns to this distinction between survival and pleasure when he distinguishes human helplessness in the face of forces of nature from the discontent of civilization. Forces of nature threaten existence; civilization threatens pleasure and sexuality (Freud 1930).

tiny], the masochist must do what is inexpedient, must act against his own interest, must ruin the prospects which open out to him in the real world and must, perhaps, destroy his own real existence" (Freud 1924, pp. 169–170). Indeed, here Freud is not only thinking of Dostoyevski's protagonists, but primarily of analysands who during the course of their psychoanalytic treatment seemingly are determined to antagonize their analyst (Freud 1914a). This way they force the analyst to adopt a cool and callous attitude toward them.[42] According to Freud, this moral masochism is an expression of an eroticized death instinct. "This moral masochism becomes a classical piece of evidence for the existence of fusion of instinct. Its danger lies in the fact that it originates from the death instinct and corresponds to that part of that instinct which has escaped being turned outwards as an instinct of destruction. But since, on the other hand, it has the significance of an erotic component, even the subject's destruction of himself cannot take place without libidinal satisfaction" (Freud 1924, p. 170). How are we to understand this?

Moral masochism shows a noticeable similarity to the compulsive repetition of traumas. The soldier who compulsively plays Russian roulette is a fitting example of someone who "must do what is inexpedient, must act against his own interest, must ruin the prospects which open out to him in the real world and must, perhaps, destroy his own real existence." Moral masochism, however, differs from the compulsion to repeat by its moral connotation. Moral masochism aims at punishment. The repetition of trauma is experienced as punishment by a parental authority. A man who again and again is abandoned by a succession of his loves appears to be under the spell of a compulsion to repeat. In these ever-returning love tragedies the primitive catastrophe of the baby abandoned by the mother is repeated. His feelings of desperation and radical dependency, which are in no relation to the situation in reality, are proof that an archaic wound has once again opened. At the same time this man experiences his misfortune in love as an act

---

42. On this point see Van Haute and Geyskens 2004.

of God or of fate. This expresses itself in his rebellious tone, interchangeable with feelings of shame about what is happening to him, as well as the bizarre conviction that he does not deserve any better. In contrast to the infernal machinations in the example of Russian roulette, the main part is here played by moral categories. In his rebelliousness and self-reproach, he appears to orient himself to a parental authority that denies him all pleasure.

This example clarifies Freud's position that moral masochism is a mixture of the death instinct and erotism. More precisely, it deals with a repetition of the primitive catastrophe of the baby as well as a repetition of the reactions of the child to the first prohibition of anal pleasure. The rebelliousness, the shame, the reference to a punishing authority all show that we are not dealing here with a pure manifestation of the death instinct. The affective reactions of the man in our example appear to be the repetition of another infantile experience than that of pure desperation and passivity. The stubbornness, the unmotivated feeling of shame, and the reference to a punishing authority, according to Freud, are modeled on the reactions of the child to the parental prohibition of anal pleasure (Freud 1905b, 1908a).

As such we are merely dealing with an analogy between the pathological reactions of an adult and the experiences of the child. But according to Freud, this analogy must be based on an underlying identity. This is where erogenous masochism comes into play. In *The Economic Problem of Masochism*, Freud claims that there is an erogenous factor at the basis of moral masochism. He says about this erogenous factor: "In my *Three Essays on the Theory of Sexuality*, in the section on the sources of infantile sexuality, I put forward the proposition that 'in the case of a great number of internal processes sexual excitation arises as a concomitant effect, as soon as the intensity of those processes passes beyond certain quantitative limits'. . . . In accordance with this, the excitation of pain and unpleasure would be bound to have the same result too" (Freud 1924, p. 163). In this discussion of the sexual excitement that occurs as a by-product of painful bodily processes, Freud, strangely enough, does not refer to his exposé of anal erotism in the *Three Essays*. Yet in his analysis of anal masturbation he explicitly referred to the mixture of pleasure and pain: "Children who make use of the susceptibility to erotogenic stimulation of the anal zone betray themselves by holding back their stool till its accumulation brings about violent muscular contractions and, as it passes through the anus, is able to produce powerful stimulation of the mucus membrane. In so doing, *it must no doubt cause not only painful but also highly pleasurable sensations*" (Freud 1905b, p. 186, italics added). It is astonishing that Freud does not make recourse to these passages about anal erotism in his descriptions of erogenous masochism. After all, Freud's description of anal erotism in 1905 seamlessly connects to his later reflections on the mingling of pleasure and pain in *The Economic Problem of Masochism.*

Freud's theory of erogenous masochism only becomes more transparent when we understand it on the basis of his earlier analysis of anal erotism. It is, after all, here that we discover a corporeal experience in which pain and erotism enter into a first conjunction. Hence we may understand anal erotism as the infantile erogenous factor in the different forms of masochism that Freud distinguishes. Perverse masochism as well as moral masochism would then be the "psychic disguises" of this original, anal-erotic *Schmerzlust* of early childhood (Freud 1924, pp. 164–165). At the same time, anal erotism offers a first modification and erotization of the mere compulsion to repeat by linking the primitive catastrophes of the baby to a parental prohibition and by ensuring that, through the anal-erotic mingling of pain and pleasure, "libidinous satisfaction is not lacking" (p. 171) in the compulsive repetition of traumas.[43]

According to Freud the parental prohibition of anal pleasure is the second great trauma of childhood after the primitive catastrophes of the baby. However, these traumas do not suffice for an adequate un-

---

43. We may find the rawest and least censured literary treatment of this problematic of moral and erogenous masochism in the Book of Job. The catastrophes that befall Job are viewed by his friends as a punishment from God. They preach either repentance or rebellion. Job rejects the "moralization" of his suffering. The text also refers to an "excremental" factor: "Skin for skin" said Satan, and afflicted Job—sitting in the ashes and mourning the loss of his children and possessions—"with painful sores from the soles of his feet to the top of his head" (Job 2:4–8).

derstanding of psychopathological phenomena, and more generally, the effects of psychic traumas. Traumas can also be disavowed. To understand this, Freud introduced the castration complex.

CASTRATION

In 1927 Freud wrote a text on fetishism. In this very short article he introduced the defense mechanism known as disavowal (*Verleugnung*). He gives the example of two brothers who had lost their father at a young age and had disavowed that fact. This means that, on the one hand, they were well aware that their father had died, while, on the other hand, not allowing that fact to get through to them, appearing to be making decisions and to be acting as if he was still alive (Freud 1927). According to Freud, this ambiguous attitude toward reality is not that uncommon in childhood, in particular with regard to sexual difference.

When the child is confronted with a demand of the instinct and with the real impossibility of, or the prohibition against, satisfying that demand, he or she can either recognize this impossibility, and forgo satisfaction, or disavow reality and maintain the satisfaction of the instinct (Freud 1940b). This situation, however, is only possible when we are dealing with a sexual instinct. In the case of a vital need, such as hunger, the child does not have a choice. It cannot but recognize the demands of the instinct. Hunger, thirst, and pain exercise an all-powerful demand. This is in contrast to the sexual instinct. Certainly in the child this instinct is not always as compelling or as urgent as other vital needs. It is less difficult for the child to give up genital masturbation than to give up food or defecation. In the case of masturbation the child therefore may opt to neglect the instinct if its satisfaction encounters difficulty. Yet what is the danger that the sexual satisfaction of the child might encounter? According to Freud this danger lies in castration. How are we to understand this?

After 1920 Freud places the castration complex more and more at the center of his theory of psychopathology and of human instinctual life in general.[44] According to Freud, neurosis, perversion, and psychosis, as well as our fear of death and the loss of love, are based on the castration complex. This is curious since the specificity of castration consists of it never having been executed. Do all our anxieties then rest on a primal fear of something that has never taken place? To understand the central role of castration in Freud's later theory, we must situate the castration complex in his theory of infantile sexuality.

During the phallic phase, that is to say in the phase in which the child is able to experience genital excitation, the genesis of sexual curiosity also takes place.[45] Through this curiosity the child is confronted with the enigmas of adult sexuality, and thus also discovers sexual difference. When the little boy discovers that there are human beings who do not have a penis, he understands sexual difference according to a binary logic. He does not think: Men have something, and women have something else. Rather, he thinks: Men have something that women do not have. He interprets female genitalia as a lack (Freud 1923). As such this does not lead to fear but rather to a feeling of male superiority regarding women. Only when the sight of human genitalia is associated with a rejection of his own genital masturbation by the parents does the phantasy of the threat of castration emerge. The sight of female genitalia informs him of the punishment that is linked to the parental rejection. Now he understands: Girls are bad boys who have been punished. Hence, the emergence of castration as a primal phantasy.

The idea of castration allows us to understand disavowal. The danger that threatens if genital masturbation is continued is castration. However, this castration is not a real danger. The danger arises

---

44. This implies that after 1920 Freud increasingly thinks of infantile sexuality from the perspective, or in function, of sexual difference and less exclusively from the view point of a "perverse" experience of pleasure on the level of the different erogenous zones. We lack the room to pursue this problematic in great detail (see Van Haute and Geyskens 2004). The fact that Klein conceives of infantile sexuality almost exclusively in terms of the Oedipus complex is a logical extension of Freud's work. We will return to this point more extensively in Chapter 2.

45. "The driving force that this male body part shall later develop in puberty, expresses itself at this stage mainly as an urge to investigate, as sexual curiosity" (Freud 1923, p. 143).

from the infantile interpretation of sexual difference. It originates in an infantile theory of sexual difference. When the little boy is now confronted with his own genital excitation he can, because of the threat of castration, either give up masturbation, or he can disavow the threat. This entails that he disavow the female genitalia, according to his theory the proof of castration (Freud 1940b, pp. 276–277). The boy maintains his previous idea that all human beings have a penis. The figure of the phallic woman emerges as a triumph over the fear of castration.

We may then ask how it is that Freud sees a connection between the boys that disavowed the death of their father and the disavowal of castration by the little boy. Freud seems to assume that disavowal is a typically male defense mechanism. After all, girls are not confronted with castration in the same manner and they derive no benefit from disavowing female genitalia. How should they be able to do that, unless they hallucinated their own penis?[46] That disavowal is indeed a typically male defense mechanism can be made plausible by a reference to sexual psychopathology. Transvestites are men who experience sexual excitement by dressing up as women and by making others believe that they really are women. In this perversion we may see a literal enactment of the phallic woman and hence disavowal of castration. Well, according to the American psychiatrist and psychoanalyst Robert Stoller, who made the study of sexual psychopathology his life work, transvestism does not occur in women. There are women who dress like men, but they then do so regularly and not in an occasional fit. They dress in male fashion but not in hyper-male fashion, and neither do they play ambiguous games with the danger of being caught (Stoller 1968).

The disavowal of a painful reality, such as, for example, death, according to Freud goes back to the infantile disavowal of castration. The boys who disavow the death of their father have learned this defense mechanism in confrontation with sexual difference. Thus

---

46. Here we cannot address the female castration complex and penis envy at length. We only report that according to Freud girls recognize sexual difference immediately. This leads to disappointment and envy, as opposed to disavowal and fear.

Freud arrives at the curious conclusion that our relation to reality is modeled on our infantile relation to a phantasy, or a theory, namely castration as the infantile interpretation of sexual difference. The disavowal of reality would then have to be an exclusively male defense mechanism. Transvestism and fetishism appear to confirm this. But is this also true for the disavowal of death and of the painful aspects of reality in general? Do women react with disappointment and envy to situations in which men react with disavowal and fear?

We have already stated that the reaction of the child to the prohibition of anal pleasure contains a modification and erotization of the mere compulsion to repeat traumas. Faced with the prohibition against attaining anal pleasure, the child may react with shame and stubbornness toward parental authority, whereas a baby cannot even react to primitive catastrophes with fear. Castration is an even further modification. The child is now able to disavow the trauma, an impossibility in the case of the preceding traumas we described. The absence of the mother cannot be disavowed by the baby because of the omnipotence of vital needs. Hunger, for example, will continue to gnaw. The threat of punishment during toilet training also cannot be disavowed because to maintain not being toilet trained will result in the loss of the love of the parents. But castration is not a real threat. It is a phantasy of the child.

In the foregoing discussion we have situated the three great traumas of childhood with respect to one another (the primitive catastrophes of the baby, the taboo of anality, and the castration). The child is utterly helpless and passive in the face of pure trauma. The prohibition of anal erotism allows for a certain reaction from the child. The child may recognize or disavow castration because within the sphere of sexuality he is able to renounce the instinct, and because castration is not a real danger but an infantile phantasy about sexual difference. This threefold trauma will be reactivated in later life in any confrontation with a painful reality. Whether we react to these painful situations by (1) repeating the trauma unmodified, (2) repeating the trauma in a mixture of pain, pleasure, and rebelliousness, or (3) disavowing reality, all depends on the force of the actual trauma, and the manner in which we were able to react as children to the threefold trauma that essentially characterized our infancy.

CONCLUSION

We have interpreted Freud's dualism of the instincts of eros and thanatos as a theory of the primacy of a vital infant trauma. In this manner Freud's theory of the death instinct implies an affirmation of the primacy of the child. Thus we arrived at the discovery of the traumatic origin of human subjectivity. The helplessness and dependency we all experienced as children repeat themselves in later situations of humiliation and loss. Freud's theory of the death instinct becomes understandable as a theory of the compulsive repetition of our infantile traumas during our later course in life.

The analysis of moral masochism and fetishism demonstrated further modifications of the original situation of radical dependency and helplessness by means of anal erotization and disavowal of sexual difference. Hence we arrived at the threefold traumatic core of the unconscious, which is not only specific for pathology, but belongs essentially to being human as such.

According to Freud, pathology is indeed merely a quantitative magnification of universal human phenomena. The infantile experiences that we may easily identify in the analyses of pathological manifestations, such as traumatic neurosis, moral masochism, and fetishism, also play a role in normality. Masochism and fetishism demonstrate the resituation of sexuality in Freud's later work. Infantile sexuality is no longer understood as the exclusively pathogenic factor, as it had been understood in Freud's earlier theory of organic repression and the pleasure principle, but on the contrary, it fulfills the function of modifying and binding more original catastrophes.

In Chapter 2 we shall investigate how we may understand Melanie Klein's theory of the paranoid-schizoid and depressive position as a clinical anthropology of fear and guilt. We shall demonstrate how in Klein's work also, fear and guilt must be conceived from a traumatic origin in the subject and hence from the primacy of the child.

2

The Death Instinct, Trauma, and Sexuality in the Work of Melanie Klein

THE DEATH INSTINCT, ANXIETY, AND GUILT

Much like in the later work of Freud, in Melanie Klein's work, too, the death instinct is central.[1] Indeed, Klein is one of the few analysts who take Freud's biological speculations about the death instinct seriously and without question. Like Freud, Klein is convinced that psychic life must be understood from the perspective of a struggle between a life instinct and a death instinct. According to her, these instincts are part of the biological equipment of humans. Furthermore, Klein thinks that the death instinct primarily takes the ego as its object.[2] From the beginning of its existence the ego is threatened by the activities of the death instinct. This explains why anxiety plays such a central role in Klein's work. The fledgling ego lives under the permanent threat of succumbing to the attacks of the death instinct. It is threatened by a force that aims at its destruction from within.[3]

The central role of the death instinct and the importance of anxiety are intrinsically linked in Kleinian metapsychology. In the first instance, anxiety is about the activities of the death instinct in the organism itself. It is the primary affect that determines the dynamics of psychic life to an important extent. This means that who I am or will be depends on the manner in which I deal with this anxiety and the aggressivity to which it

---

1. Klein relies on the texts we have discussed in the first chapter: *Beyond the Pleasure Principle* and *The Economic Problem of Masochism*. (We shall return to this point at length.)

2. This implies that Klein, in contrast to Freud, assumes that already from the beginning of existence a rudimentary ego is present. (We shall return to this point later on.)

3. This means that Klein rejects the Freudian insight that the unconscious does not know death. (We shall return to this point.)

is a response (Klein 1946). The ego must defend itself against the attacks of the death instinct and take up a position against them. According to Klein, the ego does this in directing the aggressivity outward, with the help of the life instincts, which are at the service of the ego. The aggressivity against the ego in this way is transformed into an aggressivity against an external object from which the ego at the same time fears a reaction. Will the object that I treat so aggressively not retaliate? But even though the child continues to live in a world that is dominated by anxiety and aggressivity, from now on his aggressivity is directed toward and originates in a recognizable object with regard to which I can assume a position and to which I can now relate.

Klein thinks that the primitive objects of aggressivity have a partial character. The fledgling ego does not yet relate to total objects. It lives in a world of partial objects of which the maternal breast is the paradigm. Evidently, the breast is not only an object toward which aggressivity is directed and in which it finds its origin. The breast also feeds. It satisfies the organism when it is hungry. Consequently, according to Klein, the infant is confronted with a "bad" and a "good" breast, which he or she initially experiences as two different objects. Or, to put it more precisely, the infant does everything to separate the "good" and the "bad" breast. This process of splitting, together with the idealization of the "good" breast and the disavowal of the "bad" breast (and of the painful feelings to which frustration can give rise), is one of the most archaic defense mechanisms of the ego against the anxiety of destruction. After all, the splitting enables the ego to protect the "good" breast with which it identifies against the "bad" breast, and it protects the ego from the painful confrontation with the fact that one and the same object may have "good" and "bad" sides.

Klein calls this archaic manner of dealing with anxiety characteristic of the *paranoid-schizoid position* that dominates the first months of life.[4]

---

4. For Klein, these positions have a genetic as well as a structural significance. On the one hand, they are phases of development that occur in certain moments in the history of the subject (genetic), but, on the other hand, they determine the manner in which we will deal with the anxiety and aggressivity in the further course of our lives (structural).

The experience of the child is structured at this stage by the anxiety of persecution and destruction ("paranoid"). The overwhelming role played by the process of "splitting" in this first phase of life also has as a consequence that reality as well as the ego are experienced as fragmented ("schizoid"), which further adds to the anxiety against which the self must defend itself.

This situation is only resolved with the introduction of the *depressive position* around the fourth month of life. The depressive position goes together with the modification of the original anxiety about being destroyed. In contrast to the preceding period, the child is now able to relate to a total object—in particular, to the mother—which has "good" as well as "bad" aspects. The development of its intellectual and emotional capacities implies that the child is now able to better estimate the consequences of its aggressivity toward its object. In the first instance the ego no longer fears for its own existence but for the damage that it might cause to the object on which it is dependent and that it loves. Instead of the anxiety about being destroyed, feelings of guilt about one's own aggressivity and the possible consequences dominate the experiences of the (depressive) child. New defense mechanisms now come to the fore: not splitting, but instead attempts to undo the damage (and make reparation) dominate the clinical picture.

The defense against anxiety—anxiety about destruction and the anxiety of damaging the love object—is, according to Klein, the motor of psychic life and the first task of the budding ego. Klein examines these infantile defense mechanisms from the perspective of psychopathology and more concretely that of psychoses.[5] These defense mechanisms furthermore determine the manner in which the ego will deal with anxiety and aggressivity in its later existence. This means that Klein, like Freud, understands psychic life as such relative to the tendencies and mechanisms that, if they manifest themselves unchecked, lead to pathology. Klein subscribes to the Freudian crystal principle. The pathology shows in a magnified manner the fundamental structural moments of human existence (Klein 1945). It is in this sense that

---

5. In particular, these are paranoia, schizophrenia, and melancholia (depression).

Kleinian metapsychology, like Freudian metapsychology, is a clinical anthropology.

At its core, anxiety must, according to Klein, be based on the activities of a biological death instinct. How are we to understand this? Is the Kleinian reference to the death instinct better argued than the Freudian reference that we rejected? What exactly does Klein mean when she speaks of a "bad" and a "good" breast?[6] Are we to take her pronouncements literally, or do they have a metaphorical character? And if the latter is the case, to what do these metaphors refer? If Kleinian metapsychology is a clinical anthropology, what does it then mean when Klein takes the psychoses as the most important reference point and not traumatic neuroses, as Freud does? This chapter seeks to answer these questions.

It is noteworthy how the helplessness of children toward external reality and toward their own instincts occupies a central role in Klein's theory of the death instinct (Klein 1948). We will show that the phenomena that Klein attempts to thematize on the basis of the concept of a biological death instinct can be understood without any loss of meaning in terms of the essential and radical helplessness of the child. Like the Freudian theory of the death instinct, the Kleinian theory is a biological metaphor that refers to the traumatic core of the unconscious and of subjectivity. In Klein, just as in Freud, this trauma is situated beyond the pleasure principle and sexuality. Yet there is an important difference. To the primary trauma that Freud speaks of, no answer is possible. In the most literal sense of the term, the infant is defenseless against it. However, the child is not powerless against the Kleinian trauma. From the outset, children already dispose of different defense mechanisms that allow them to deal with trauma. Consequently, Freudian trauma cannot simply be equated with the Kleinian trauma. We will link the different formulations of the primary trauma in Freud and Klein with the fact that in their reflections both take their start in a different

---

6. Or, for example, as we shall address later in great detail, when she speaks about poisoned excrement with which the small child attacks its mother and so forth?

pathology. Freud's starting point is traumatic neurosis, while Klein's is the different psychotic pathologies.[7]

Klein orders the primitive defense mechanisms of the ego in light of two positions: the paranoid-schizoid position and the depressive position.[8] These defense mechanisms have a "phantasmatic" character. Consequently we must ask not only how these positions are to be understood and how they relate to one another, but also what exactly Klein means when she calls them "phantasmatic." We will see how the Kleinian concept of phantasy must at the same time be called an original concept of corporeality, which differs substantially from the Freudian one.

In the previous chapter we saw how in his later texts Freud understands the significance of sexuality for human existence more and more in relation to the need of the psyche to deal with a primitive trauma. In a certain sense this is no different in Klein's work. She posits that the development of the psyche must not so much be understood from the point of sexuality but rather on the basis of two fundamental positions. Sexual development is subordinate to, while at the same time playing an important role in, the working through of infantile (psychotic) anxieties (Klein 1952).[9] At the same time, sexuality is completely, or at least strongly, oedipalized, which means that it must be thought of according to the model of adult sexuality and the primacy of the genital libido. This is Klein's answer to Freud's tendency in his later texts to thematize sexuality more and more from the perspective

---

7. In the background a problem is at work to which clinical anthropology is yet to give an answer: Is the way in which it articulates the fundamental structures of subjectivity not directly dependent on the pathologies in which it takes its starting point, such that its claims are inevitably whimsical? Why should one, after all, give preference to psychoses above traumatic neuroses in order to uncover the essential structures of subjectivity? In our conclusion we will return to this problematic more extensively.

8. Even though the problematic of both of these positions is already present in Klein's work from very early on, she only introduces the depressive position explicitly in 1935 and the paranoid-schizoid position in 1946.

9. We will return to the relation of infantile psychotic anxieties and psychosis in the psychiatric sense of the term.

of or in function of sexual difference. We discuss this problematic in the last paragraph of this chapter. Let us, however, first return to the problem of the status of trauma in the work of Klein.[10]

THE TRAUMATIC ORIGIN OF SUBJECTIVITY IN THE WORK OF KLEIN

Klein's Study of Little Dick

Very early on, Klein's clinical work taught her that infantile anxieties go together with sadistic impulses and phantasies. Hence already in an early study on "The Importance of Symbol-Formation in the Development of the Ego" (Klein 1932), she discusses the relation between little Dick's inability to relate to his surrounding reality and the other in a meaningful manner and his aggressive impulses, in particular toward his mother. What is immediately noticeable in Klein's observations of Dick is the absence of any anxiety and the absence of any contact. Dick does not seek contact. In no way does he appeal to the other or to reality. He lives, says Klein, in a reality without depth that does not appear to appeal to his imagination in any way. It is an unsymbolized reality without significance, in which also the therapist [Melanie Klein] is nothing more than just another piece of furniture. Dick does not show any desire to express himself or to make himself understood by others.

Klein emphasizes the link between the absence of anxiety in Dick and the fact that he lives in an undifferentiated reality—an "unreal reality," as she puts it (Klein 1932, p. 221). The reality in which we pursue

---

10. We ground our exposition of Klein on her later texts in particular: *A Contribution to the Psychogenesis of Manic-Depressive States* (1935), *Love, Guilt, and Reparation* (1937), *Mourning and Its Relation to Manic-Depressive States* (1940), *The Oedipus Complex in the Light of Early Anxieties* (1945), *Notes on Some Schizoid Mechanisms* (1946), *On the Theory of Anxiety and Guilt* (1948), and *Some Theoretical Conclusions Regarding the Emotional Life of the Infant* (1952). For a discussion of the development of Kleinian thought, we refer to the literature, in particular Segal (1964, 1979), Petot (1990), Meltzer (1994), Hinshelwood (1994), and Likierman (2001).

our existence normally consists of objects to which we are related affectively, which interest us, and which are also linked among one another in many often surprising ways. The latter is not the case with Dick. From this perspective, he does not really live in a human world. First we shall ask how this human world full of meaning comes to be, according to Klein.

In this context, Klein refers to the decisive role of the oral sadistic phase of the development of the libido (Klein 1930). In this phase the instinct is characterized by the desire to master the contents of the mother's body—the penis of the father (or his entire body), excrements, and other children[11]—and the desire to destroy her with all the means at the disposal of sadism. The oral sadistic phase is at the same time the first introduction to the Oedipus complex. From now on, the genital impulses will make their influence felt. In the phantasies of this period, the excrements are transformed, according to Klein, into dangerous weapons, or into poisonous substances, and the attacks on the mother's body and its contents play a central role. This sadistic excess also inevitably leads to anxiety and to the need to defend oneself against it. After all, young children fear being repaid in kind by the objects that they treat so cruelly. The oral-sadistic introjection of objects that is characteristic for this period of mental development consequently leads to an internalization of this anxiety,[12] which threatens to inundate the young child's as yet barely developed ego. The young child may defend himself by projecting these objects back upon the outside. For our problematic, the following is important. The anxiety of retaliation by the primary object (breast, penis, the vagina, and so forth) causes the young child, accord-

---

11. How we are to understand these enigmatic insights will be dealt with in the paragraphs that follow. For the time being we will simply adopt Klein's use of language and remark that Klein warns continually that her descriptions of the infantile experience exclusively refer to their content but say nothing about the form in which these phantasies occur (Klein 1945). One must be wary of thinking of these phantasies according to the model of (visual) phantasies in adults.

12. By this Klein also means that the small child, as it were, literally takes the objects by which he or she feels attacked and on which he or she directs aggressivity, for example, the breast, into oneself. Consequently, the danger no longer comes exclusively "from the outside" but now also threatens the child from the inside. How these processes are to be understood exactly can only become apparent in our further exposition.

ing to Klein, to equate these organs and objects with other objects in the external world, which are linked in the child's imagination with the original objects, but which evoke less anxiety. The space between two doors, for example, may represent the mother's body, or a toy train may represent the father. These new objects are not only taken up in the world of experience of the child but they become objects of anxiety that once again force the child to make new equations and identifications. The defense against anxiety and the metonymical constitution of a human—in the first instance merely phantastic—reality thus go hand in hand in Klein's work.

It appears to be exactly this process that did not develop or developed insufficiently in Dick. Dick is not able to deal with anxiety and hence does not make symbolic (as Klein puts it) equations between objects. He thus continues to live in a meaningless and gray universe. Klein links this with the premature entry into the genital phase by which Dick's penis became the most important organ of his sadism and, in particular, with the premature acquisition of defense mechanisms characteristic of this phase. Aggressive phantasies—for example, Dick lifts a toy to his mouth and says "tea (eat) daddy," with which he is supposed to indicate his desire to introject the father's penis and remove it from the body of the mother—according to Klein are not only linked with the anxiety of retaliation but at the same time with feelings of guilt and compassion and the feeling of having to repair the damage caused. The distinction between the schizoid-paranoid position and the depressive position that Klein will develop later already plays a clear background role.[13] However, we will not concern ourselves with this problematic here. The following is important for us now. According to Klein we are dealing in the case of Dick with a premature development of the ego that makes feelings of guilt possible as well as a relation of empathy to the object of aggressivity, but

---

13. As we have already mentioned, the anxiety about one's own existence is characteristic of the schizoid-paranoid position, and feelings of guilt and anxiety about the damage that the object is supposed to have suffered are characteristic of the depressive position.

at the same time blocks any further development of the ego.[14] Dick's premature capacity for empathy with the object of his aggressivity does indeed compel him to defend massively against his aggressive impulses. He does this, writes Klein, by identifying in an exaggerated manner with the object—the mother—or, which according to Klein clearly amounts to the same thing, by withdrawing phantasmatically into the empty dark body of the mother. In this way Dick succeeds in separating himself from reality and his mother and in protecting her against his aggressive impulses. At the same time, however, he loses any interest in an affective link to his (real) mother, and to significant others in general.

The case study of Dick illustrates the complex connection of the problematic of anxiety and aggressivity in Klein's work and the great importance she assigns to a good understanding of early childhood. Anxiety is essentially about (the consequences of) aggressivity. But how may we explain the presence of sadistic impulses in the small child? Where do they come from and why do they play such a prominent role in the infantile world of experience? It is at this point of the argument that Klein introduces the hypothesis of a biological death instinct.[15]

A Death Instinct, or the Primacy of Trauma?

Klein introduces the death instinct in order to give an account of the decisive role of sadistic phantasies and the anxieties they are linked with in the infantile world of experience, as well as the intensity of these

---

14. We will return to this case study in the paragraph on sexuality in the work of Klein. The anxieties linked to Dick's genital tendencies also lead to the repression of the oedipal problematic.

15. "Some years later—that is, after the publication of 'The Importance of Symbol-Formation in the Development of the Ego'—in my attempt to reach a fuller understanding of infantile sadistic phantasies and their origin, I was led to apply Freud's hypothesis of the struggle between the life and death instincts to the clinical material gained in the analysis of young children" (Klein 1948, p. 28).

anxieties.[16] We recall that according to Freud the death instinct is at work in nature as a whole. In this sense Freud's texts on the death instinct are speculations on the philosophy of nature. This is far less explicitly the case in Klein. She merely wishes to gain insight into her clinical data. Consequently she only pursues the death instinct to the extent that she perceives it to be at work in the human organism.

If, as Freud (1924) claims, the death instinct is at work in the organism from the beginning of its existence, then the awareness of death must, according to Klein, also be present from the very beginning. "Following this line of thought"—namely Freud's reflections on the death instinct—"I put forward the hypothesis that anxiety is aroused by the danger which threatens the organism from the death instinct; and I suggested that this is the primary cause of anxiety" (Klein 1948, p. 28).[17] According to Klein, the anxiety of death is the most fundamental form of anxiety.

Klein assumes that the activity of the death instinct confronts the child with the anxiety of being destroyed. According to her, this anxiety is not exclusively the consequence of frustrations—such as the absence of food or of oxygen—with which the child is inevitably also confronted (Klein 1948). On the contrary, Klein thinks that the intensity of the infantile situations of anxiety that she encounters in her clinical practice cannot be explained by such frustrations alone. These situations demand a further foundation in a death instinct that threatens and attacks the organism and the fledgling ego from within.

---

16. Evidently the infantile situations of anxiety that Klein was able to observe in her practice did not permit a direct perception of the death instinct. Klein, for example, interprets the anxiety about being eaten by the father as an unambiguous expression of the anxiety about the total destruction of the self. According to Klein, this anxiety is itself the consequence of the projection of the aggressive impulses of the infant on its object. Klein writes that in this way the breast of the mother and the mother herself are transformed into voracious objects in the infantile phantasy. This anxiety quickly extends to encompass the father's penis (Klein 1948). We will still return to the question of how to understand these (at first sight curious) pronouncements.

17. Elsewhere Klein writes: "I would also think that if we assume the existence of a death instinct, we must also assume that in the deepest layer of the mind there is a response to this instinct in the form of fear of annihilation of life" (Klein 1948, p. 29).

We know that Freud himself never drew this conclusion. For Freud, the most fundamental anxiety of the child is the anxiety of castration and not the anxiety of destruction. The adult's anxiety of death must be understood in light of the infantile anxiety of castration. The infantile relation to this phantasy of castration, according to Freud, determines our adult relation to death. As Freud sees it, the unconscious does not know death. Anxiety of death as such cannot cause neurosis, because we have no mental representation of death (Freud 1926). We have, however, also already suggested that the absence of a concrete idea of death only increases its anxiety-inducing characteristic. What we can represent to ourselves is an identifiable danger against which we can at least nurture the illusion of being able to defend ourselves.[18] Let us take the example of a child who is very hungry. When this feeling of hunger crosses a certain threshold, it may be experienced as a threat to life itself. We may imagine that this child feels his existence to be threatened from within and starts to panic. But panic in view of what? In any case, it is not a panic concerning something of which the child can form a concrete representation. It only experiences in his own body that his existence is threatened. Or picture someone who is on the verge of drowning. What is this person afraid of? It is death, the immanent character of which the person experiences, without having to have a concrete idea thereof. Anxiety of death is not primarily of the order of representation. It is, as it were, experienced on the level of the body itself as "a nameless dread" (Bion 1962).[19]

We are now in a position further to specify the contrast between Freud and Klein regarding the relation between the unconscious and death. According to Freud, the unconscious is primarily of the order

---

18. This is also the reason why Klein reverses the relation between the anxiety of death and the anxiety of castration. The anxiety of castration is a concretization of, and protection against, the anxiety of death. Castration, after all, is also a threat to our corporeal integrity, but we are dealing here with a threat of which we have a concrete mental image and against which we can protect ourselves (Klein 1948). We shall return to this point.

19. This appears to imply that Klein uses the panic attack as the model for her conception of anxiety.

of representation. Only what can be represented has a concrete psychic content (Freud 1926). Hence, concerning the hypothesis of the trauma of birth, Freud writes that in spite of the child at the moment of birth being inundated by unpleasurable stimuli we may in no way link this with awareness or knowledge of a (possible) destruction of life (Freud 1926). The newborn child, after all, is not capable of forming a mental representation of death. Undoubtedly this insight is connected with Freud's hypothesis that the ego is not present from the outset. According to Freud, the ego is a psychic acquisition. It is not innate but only comes to be in the course of psychic development (Freud 1914b).[20] At the same time, Freud (1926) and Klein (1948) agree that the ego is the seat of anxiety. It is the place in which anxiety is experienced as psychologically significant. The initial absence of the ego and of a developed ability for representation implies for Freud that the situations of anxiety from earliest childhood can only be described in economic terms[21] as an increase in tension, without a psychic working-through.[22]

According to Klein, by contrast, we are all born with a rudimentary ego. As such the ego is not a psychic acquisition; it is given from the beginning onward. The way in which it develops, but not its origin, can become the object of psychoanalytic investigation. Hence from the beginning onward there is also a psychic instance that experiences the activities of the death instinct and that can be anxious for its bare existence. At the same time, Klein rejects, albeit implicitly, Freud's assumption that only what can be represented can have a psychic significance. According

---

20. The impossibility of the child reacting to the first trauma, not even with anxiety, is also connected with Freud's idea that the ego only comes to be during the course of further development.

21. Laplanche and Pontalis (1967) define this economic point of view as follows: it "qualifies everything having to do with the hypothesis that psychical processes consist in the circulation and distribution of an energy (instinctual energy) that can be quantified, i.e. capable of increase, decrease, and equivalence" (p. 127).

22. This is probably the reason why Freud's descriptions of the death instinct and its vicissitudes in *Beyond the Pleasure Principle* and *The Economic Problem of Masochism* often appear so abstract and so far removed from the concrete experience of a concrete subject. On this point see The First Taboo in Chapter 1 of this volume.

to Klein, corporeal experience is immediately meaningful and therefore does not require the detour via representation. Anxiety of death is not the anxiety of something that we have a representation of, it is a feeling of threat that comes to exist and is experienced in the body itself.[23]

When we try to imagine the concrete forms in which the primary anxiety of destruction occurs, then we must primarily picture the helplessness of the small child with regard to internal and external threats (Klein 1948). Children who are hungry cannot remove this unpleasant feeling on their own. They are completely delivered over to their environment for the stilling of this hunger. One may imagine, Klein continues, that children might experience their surrounding reality as hostile or have the feeling that their surroundings are not positively inclined toward them if the feeling of hunger is not immediately assuaged with an offering of food. We are dealing here as little with a concrete representation of a concrete danger as we were in the case of the anxiety of death. Rather, we must think that the reality receives a hostile shade in an undifferentiated manner. "It" is hostile toward me. Klein concludes that the experience of helplessness makes external reality appear hostile, together with the first object—the breast.

It is evident that what Klein here calls the breast must not be thought of as an already well-distinguished object of which the child has a visual representation. The breast we are dealing with is rather a proto-object that coincides with the pleasurable or unpleasurable experience of the child on the level of the oral zone. The oral zone is a zone of exchange with the external world. It is the place via which food is taken in and spat out. The young child does not yet have an articulated representation of the breast that gives this food. For children it is just a feeling of fulfillment that they have when they are fed, or the painful stimulus that they experience in their innermost being, for example, together with the feeling of dehydration in the mouth when they are hungry or thirsty.[24] The reference to a first object here primarily means the hostile or benign character of the external world we described

---

23. The full implications of this standpoint will only become apparent later on.

24. In the first case Klein speaks of the "good" breast, in the second of the "bad" breast. We shall return to this point.

as receiving a minimal localization in relation to a specific zone of the body that is primarily a locus of exchange with the surrounding reality.[25]

The appearance of the first object, according to Klein, coincides with the redirection of the death instinct onto the external world under the influence of the life instincts. The death instinct is no longer primarily directed onto the ego but toward an external object. The death instinct now shows itself as aggressivity toward the object that denies the child satisfaction. Not only is this redirection the first defense mechanism of the ego against the anxiety of being destroyed by the internal activity of the death instinct, but, according to Klein, it also contributes to the fact that the reality is experienced as hostile. When I direct my aggressivity onto an external object, will it not wish to retaliate in kind (Klein 1948)?

We have already pointed out that Klein does not situate this entire dynamics in the helplessness of the child as such or in the frustrations of which it inevitably becomes the victim but in the activities of a hypothetical death instinct. Helplessness only contributes to the overwhelming character of the anxiety of being destroyed. In the same vein, Klein (1948) writes that the painful experience of birth reinforces the paranoia that originates in the activity of the death instinct, but does not cause it. Painful experiences and frustration do indeed contribute to primitive anxiety, but this anxiety can ultimately not be founded upon them. Properly speaking it is the opposite: the first frustrations contribute to a solution for this anxiety. They are, after all, what allows us to direct the death instinct outward (Heimann 1952).

How plausible is Klein's reference to a biological death instinct? Or, put otherwise, how necessary is the reference to a biological force that threatens the ego from within in order to understand the experiences to which Klein refers? We already know that Klein legitimizes its introduction on the basis of the intensity of infantile anxiety situations. Another important motive is nevertheless in play. In the previous chapter, we described the Freudian death instinct as the result of a confusion of

---

25. The zones to which Klein refers in this context are, in truth, the erogenous zones that Freud speaks about. We shall return to this point in great detail when discussing the place and significance of these zones in Kleinian metapsychology.

tongues: from the demonic character of repetition Freud deduces that it has an instinctual character and must hence have a biological origin. It appears that the same confusion of tongues is at work in the thought of Klein. The primitive anxiety to be destroyed, she writes, is never completely eliminated and remains active—repeats itself—in all later situations of anxiety. This repetition lends anxiety the appearance of being instinctual, which would justify the introduction of a biological death instinct. As we did with Freud hitherto, we must ask the question of whether we are not dealing with a superfluous biologization of the problematic of repetition.

It is noteworthy that several students of Klein as well as Klein herself sometimes leave aside references to the death instinct in their descriptions of the primitive anxiety of death. Klein, for example, writes, "I have put forward the hypothesis that the newborn baby experiences, both in the process of birth and in the adjustment to the postnatal situation, anxiety of a persecutory nature. This can be explained by the fact that the young infant, without it being able to grasp it intellectually, feels unconsciously every discomfort as though it were inflicted on him by hostile forces" (Klein 1959, p. 248). Joan Rivière (1952) is of the opinion that the helplessness and the dependency of the small child compel us to assume that the infant knows the anxiety of death. Isaacs (1948) also posits that painful experiences form the basis for phantasies of hostile internal and external objects and that they contribute to an important extent to their formation. These statements appear to go against Klein's basic tenet that primitive anxieties cannot be understood apart from the activities of the death instinct. It is precisely for this reason, however, that these passages do indicate how we may reformulate Kleinian thought, omitting the death instinct (which from a biological point of view is highly improbable) but including its most fundamental intuitions.

Let us imagine a child who for the first time is hungry and exposed to the painful internal stimuli that go along with it. This hypothetical small child does not know how he has to react to these stimuli and is in any case not really able to do so. Put still more forcefully, in principle the child does not even know whether these painful stimuli will ever disappear or whether he will be helped in an adequate manner. One may imagine that such an experience evokes anger and aggressivity. But what should this anger and aggressivity be directed toward? Adults, too, are familiar with the experience of being swamped by anger and aggressivity to such an extent that they cannot but shout: "I'm going to explode!" Does this not refer to the fact that this anger is also experienced as a threat to one's own self? And is this not all the more the case for the small child who does not (quite yet) know where it can direct this aggressivity? More so than in the adult, this aimless anger and aggressivity are experienced as a threat to one's own self that has the feeling that one will explode under the pressure of the aggressivity that one doesn't know how to deal with.[26] Together with the frustrations to which the child is subject, this explains the primitive anxiety of being destroyed by an internal force against which the child must defend by directing it outward. In this way the primitive anxiety that Klein speaks of can be reconstructed without any reference to a biological death instinct.

Our reinterpretation of the Kleinian death instinct, like our reinterpretation of the Freudian death instinct, leads to an affirmation of the primacy of the child. At the origin of our existence we must postulate a primitive and structural trauma that is intrinsically interwoven with the helplessness of the infant. Like the Freudian death instinct, the Kleinian death instinct refers to a situation of radical helplessness, from which no one escapes. This helplessness, and the anxiety that accompanies it, according to Klein, is helplessness toward one's own instincts, more precisely, toward one's own aggressivity. This original anxiety is never entirely eliminated: all later anxieties are a working through and repetition of the original helplessness (Klein 1948). This implies that the original trauma must also, according to Klein, be situated in the sphere of vital needs and not in that of sexuality.

---

26. The following quote from Rivière (1936) appears to support our interpretation: "If the desired breast is not forthcoming and the baby's aggressivity develops to the limits of its bodily capacities, this discharge which automatically follows upon a painful sensation itself produces unpleasure in the highest degree. The child is overwhelmed by choking; its eyes are blinded with tears, its ears deafened, its throat sore; its bowels gripe, its evacuations burn, the aggressive anxiety reaction is far too strong a weapon in the hands of such a weak ego; it has become uncontrollable and is threatening to destroy its owner" (p. 34). The threatening character of aggressivity must furthermore be linked to the fact that the early ego is not yet highly integrated (Klein 1946).

Trauma and Helplessness in Freud and Klein

Although we now seem to have returned to a Freudian position, there are nevertheless important differences between the Freudian and Kleinian theory of an original trauma. Freud links the original trauma with the helplessness and radical passivity of the child. However, with respect to the Kleinian trauma the child is not powerless and does not remain passive. The fundamental reason for this is that Freud addresses infantile helplessness on the basis of a reflection on traumatic neurosis, while Klein takes her starting point from the problematic of psychosis. What does this mean?

Let us recall that Freud introduces an original infantile trauma in order to explain the compulsion to repeat proper to the clinical picture of traumatic neurosis. Freud identifies the infantile factor at the basis of traumatic neurosis as a universal experience of radical dependency. But the problematic of traumatic neuroses implies that no response is possible for this first trauma. Exactly because the child can in no way answer or react to the original trauma, it must repeat it. Freud postulates the radical passivity of the child in order to clarify the traumatic neuroses that constitute his starting point. Furthermore, this passivity is even more radical since Freud assumes that the ego is not given from the outset and that therefore there is no psychic instance that can deal with trauma or react to it. Consequently, Freud's way of understanding primitive trauma coincides with the starting point of his clinical anthropology and as such is intrinsically interwoven with the clinical problematic that he wishes to clarify.

In contrast to Freud, Klein's interest does not lie in explaining traumatic neuroses, but rather the various psychotic pathologies that she is confronted with in her clinical practice—in adults as well as in children.[27] Like Freud she is convinced that such an explanation is only possible if we can determine the infantile factor at the basis of these

---

27. "The hypotheses I shall put forward, which relate to very early stages of development, are derived by inference from the material in the analyses of adults and children, and some of these hypotheses seem to tally with observations familiar in psychiatric work" (Klein 1946, p. 1).

pathologies.[28] Unlike the traumatized subject, the psychotic patient does not suffer reality passively. The psychotic subject is delivered into the hands of unspeakable anxieties but it creatively transforms reality by means of delusions and hallucinations. This appears to be the ultimate reason why Klein perceives the infantile trauma in a different way than Freud does.[29] The original trauma cannot be totally alien to the problematic that it must help to clarify. If this problematic is characterized by anxieties and a (hyper)creative dealing with reality, then we must also be able to find something of it back in the traumatic situation to which it is linked. With Klein, too, the way in which the primitive trauma is thematized is intrinsically interwoven with the clinical problematic she wishes to elucidate.

Klein bases her reflections on the death instinct mainly on *The Economic Problem of Masochism* and also on *Beyond the Pleasure Principle*. In Chapter 1 we demonstrated that Freud's theory of erogenous masochism only becomes transparent if we understand it on the basis of an analysis of anal erotism and the parental prohibition of anal pleasure. We referred to the latter as the second great trauma of childhood. Anal erotism is the erogenous factor in the various forms of masochism distinguished by Freud. At the same time anal erotism offers the first modification and erotization of the mere compulsion to repeat: the catastrophes of the baby are now related to a parental prohibition to which the child can react and the anal-erotic intermingling of pleasure and pain allows for the possibility of libidinous sat-

---

28. This also explains the debate between Anna Freudians and Kleinians. In contrast to Klein, Anna Freud posits that a pedagogical intervention is necessary in the therapy with children because the superego of the child is not yet fully formed (A. Freud 1914, p. 130). For Anna Freud, this means that the infantile factor on the basis of which adult pathologies must be understood—the Oedipus complex—has not yet fully crystallized in her little patients. Infantile pathology consequently has a different status than adult pathology. It cannot be understood on the basis of an infantile factor. Since Klein also links the psychopathology of children with an infantile factor, its status does not differ in essence from the psychopathology of adults. Infantile pathologies can be treated in a completely analogous manner—that is to say, without any pedagogical correction.

29. Probably this is also the reason why Klein, unlike Freud, presupposes that the ego is present from the beginning.

isfaction in the compulsive repetition of traumas. Even though the Kleinian trauma is not simply identical to the second great trauma of childhood Freud describes,[30] what Klein calls the original trauma nevertheless has to be situated formally on the level of Freud's second trauma. In both cases, after all, we are dealing with a trauma to which the subject can react. For Freud this already implies modification of a first trauma to which no answer was possible. This is not the case with Klein.

How does the Kleinian subject respond to trauma? We have already pointed out that in the first instance young children direct the death instinct—and their own aggressivity, with which they react to their own helplessness—outward in order to defend against it. In the same process this aggressivity is linked to an object—the breast—that from now on functions as the external representative of the aggressivity (Klein 1948). But how does the subject relate to this object? How does it deal with the anxiety that this object evokes? Before we give an answer to this question, we briefly identify the paths along which aggressivity is directed toward the outside. This problematic involves the meaning of erogenous zones in Kleinian metapsychology. At the same time it implies a reformulation of the Freudian theory of anaclisis (*Anlehnung*) of sexuality.

A Theory of Anaclisis of Aggressivity?

In *Three Essays on the Theory of Sexuality*, Freud (1905b) writes extensively on the various characteristics of infantile sexuality. According to Freud, the most important characteristics of infantile sexuality are the following: it originates in erogenous zones, it comes to exist by leaning on the satisfaction of vital functions, and it is essentially autoerotic. The infantile instinct originates in different erogenous zones (mouth, anus, etc.) that are situated all over the body. These zones are

---

30. For example, erogenous masochism in Freud is concerned with anal erotism, whereas Klein appears to defend a primacy of orality; we shall return to this point.

the privileged places of exchange with the outside world and fulfill a crucial role in the satisfaction of the vital needs of the child. At the same time they are privileged places of the experience of pleasure (and hence *erogenous* zones).

In this context, Freud (1905b) writes that sexuality emerges as an independent instinct anaclitically to the satisfaction of vital functions. In the beginning the instinct of self-preservation and the sexual instinct are intermingled: the satisfaction of the first is essentially linked to the satisfaction of the second. The feeding of the small child, for example, goes together with an experience of pleasure in the mouth that cannot simply be reduced to the (functional) pleasure it gains from the satisfaction of this specific need. In other words, feeding goes together with an experience of pleasure that cannot be reduced to the pleasure that the child experiences in the satisfaction of the need for food. Both types of pleasure must be distinguished from one another, since the pleasure in a second phase is pursued for the sake of itself, apart from any vital need. Sucking one's thumb is a fitting example. According to Freud, children try to repeat the pleasure they already experienced while being fed, but now without any vital need. Entirely analogously, for example, washing of the anal zone and the satisfaction of excremental functions may give rise to pleasurable stimuli that the young child, separate from any hygienic function or vital need, may seek to repeat (anal masturbation). According to Freud this is the moment at which the sexual instinct becomes independent. The sexual instinct does not come into existence on the occasion of finding an adequate object (such as, for example, the breast as the object of oral libido) but when the object is lost. Put differently, sexuality originates as an independent instinct anaclitically (*Anlehnung*) to the satisfaction of a vital need and at the moment that the real object is abandoned, or, which amounts to the same thing, at the moment that the instinct becomes autoerotic. Up until that point, the sexual instinct cannot be distinguished from the instinct of self-preservation.

We must further add on this point that there can be no doubt that for Freud "erogenous" means the same as "sexual." Oral, anal, and other infantile experiences of pleasure may after all be found in adult sexuality as intermediary sexual goals (kissing, looking, etc.). For Freud it is certain that these activities can only be included in adult sexuality to the extent that the infantile forms of the experience of pleasure that are thus being repeated already had a sexual character. The tree is recognized by its fruit. Just as apple seeds can produce an apple tree only because they already contain all that is necessary for it, the infantile experience of pleasure at the erogenous zones can only become sexual, according to Freud, because it had already always been so from the outset.[31]

Klein adopts Freud's theory of erogenous zones, but modifies it at the same time. She agrees with Freud that they are privileged zones of the experience of pleasure, but does not concern herself, or at least troubles much less, with the possible sexual character of this pleasure.[32] At the same time, she stresses that they are zones of exchange with the outside world, and places a greater emphasis than Freud on the bodily activities that take place in these zones: the oral zone is the zone in which the small child actively takes in food and spits it out. The taking in and spitting out of food is furthermore linked with painful or pleasurable stimuli in the digestive tract, which must also be considered in the problematic of erogenous zones. Indeed, Freud does not deny this, but he is less interested than Klein is in the activities that take place in the systems (for example, the alimentary canal) to which the erogenous zones belong. It is precisely this interest that allows Klein to reformulate Freud's theory of anaclisis of sexuality.

Klein presupposes an archaic experience in which the corporeal and the psychic are not yet differentiated.[33] These distinctions are

---

31. For a more elaborate commentary on this problematic see Van Haute and Geyskens 2004. There one may also find a further account of the fact that Freud calls every erogenous experience of pleasure sexual. On this topic see also Geyskens 2005.

32. We will return in more depth to the status of sexuality in Klein's work.

33. Here too Klein's starting point is psychosis. It has become common knowledge that in psychosis, and particularly in schizophrenia, words lose their metaphorical force, and inscribe themselves directly in the body. One famous example is Freud's patient who feared that her eyes were "twisted" (Freud 1905b). Freud links this to the fact that she calls her lover a fraud (*Augenverdreher*—literally, eye-twister). Another example is a patient who feared that her hands were cut off since she was "handicapped"

characteristic for adults. They structure the adult experience of itself and of reality, but according to Klein (1945), are not yet applicable to the infant (Isaacs 1948). The distinctions among sensation, corporeal stimulus, affect and psychic meaning are not yet present at the beginning of human existence and are only differentiated later on. According to Klein, hungry children have sensations in their mouth, lips, and intestines that immediately signify what is being done to them, or that they are doing what they desire or fear at a given moment (Isaacs 1948). In this context we have already pointed out that the "good" or "bad" breast is just an inner feeling of fullness or emptiness (pain), which immediately has a particular significance[34] without—and this is the key—it being possible to distinguish significance from sensation. The corporeal experience is therefore immediately significant or institutes significance.[35] In contrast to Freud, for Klein the body is not, in the first instance, a "machine of pleasure" but rather a "machine of significance."[36]

(Moyaert 1981). These examples all have in common that the body has become the place where the meaning of words is expressed directly. In a somewhat analogous manner, the psychotic subject may experience all sorts of strange sensations in its body, which are then immediately significant to it (for example, "a strange power is taking possession of me"). Here too there is no longer any distance between the body and significance. For the psychotic subject it is not *as if* a strange power possesses it. On the contrary, a strange sensation means that *immediately* this is the case. For Klein it is evident that this immediate fusion of the corporeal and the psychic that characterizes psychosis entails recourse to the infantile experience of the body that is analogous to it (Hinshelwood 1994). The significance of corporeality must primarily be understood from the perspective of pathology.

34. In what follows we shall see that Klein identifies this significance with phantasy; we shall return to this point.

35. This theory inevitably recalls Merleau-Ponty's (1945) notion of the corporeal subject. To develop this problematic further here would lead us too far astray.

36. Various psychoanalytic theories can be distinguished from one another on the basis of their different concepts of corporeality. For Freud the body is in the first instance a machine of pleasure. In this sense Freud adheres to a hedonistic concept of the body. Klein, in contrast, places much more emphasis on the body as the origin of meaning. In a somewhat provocative fashion we might here speak of a "hermeneutic" concept of the body. Lacan's insights concerning the real body of the drive, on the other hand, rather refer to the traumatic aspects of corporeality, or even better, to the body of the drive as trauma (Declerq 2000).

We have referred to erogenous zones as places of exchange (pleasurable or not) with the external world. They are places at which the body opens and closes intermittently in the exercise of vital functions and activities that affect the body most profoundly. These activities go together with pleasurable as well as unpleasurable stimuli. Thus we may understand why the erogenous zones are, for Klein, the places where the aggressive instinct is directed toward the outside in a privileged fashion, and in which way this occurs. Since sensation and significance are not yet differentiated for the infant, aggressive instincts (for example, evoked by frustration) may find immediate expression—or, which amounts to the same thing, may have an immediate psychic equivalent—in unpleasurable corporeal experiences. Klein writes, for example, how bed-wetting (enuresis) must be linked to powerful phantasies about the harmful effects of urine and the dangers associated with it. This does not mean that children have concrete and conceptual ideas of the harmfulness of urine. On the contrary, while wetting their bed they have unpleasurable corporeal experiences, which cannot be distinguished from the belief in the harmfulness of urine. The experiences are one and the same as this belief. Also, when Klein writes, for example, that children project the bad breast outward in order to protect themselves against the internal attacks of which they feel themselves to be the victim, we must understand this in a concrete "corporeal" manner.[37] When children vomit they have any number of unpleasurable sensations that are not all that different from the belief that they attack the "bad" breast (a "badness" they feel within themselves), when evacuating it from their body. The anger that children feel because of the frustration they suffer finds immediate expression in the unpleasurable sensations that accompany these frustrations and the associated corporeal reaction. Even though Klein is not concerned with the question of how aggressivity may detach itself from the instinct of self-preservation, we feel we are justified in speaking of a theory of

---

37. We write "corporeality" in quotation marks because we are not dealing with the organic body that biology speaks of, but with the body that institutes significance. In this way we must understand that all psychic mechanisms (introjection, projection, splitting, etc.) have their primal model, as it were, in concrete corporeal processes from which they may initially hardly be distinguished.

anaclisis of aggressivity. Aggressivity is directed toward the outside anaclitically to the exercise of concrete vital processes and functions for which the erogenous zones act as points of passage.[38]

In this context Klein does, however, affirm a primacy of orality. "The destructive impulse projected outwards is first experienced as oral aggressivity" (Klein 1946, p. 5).[39] The oral zone does indeed play a crucial role in the first exchanges with the external world. The first thing a child must do is to survive, and naturally, food intake is of decisive importance for the child as well as for the adult caregiver.[40] Frustrating as well as pleasurable contacts with the external world in a first moment are indeed made in the oral zone, perhaps not exclusively but certainly to a privileged extent. This makes it comprehensible why Klein states that destructive impulses are first experienced as oral aggressivity.

We now know how the aggressivity with which children react to their helplessness is projected outward, according to Klein.[41] This transfer of aggressivity to objects in the external world is a defensive mechanism against the anxiety that is provoked by aggressivity and more particularly by the death instinct. Through this transfer the aggressivity is linked to an object—the breast—that forthwith functions as its external representative. This object now becomes the primary source of the anxiety against which infants must defend themselves, and with which they have to learn to cope.

---

38. "My argument in this paper is based on the assumption that there is an early stage of mental development at which sadism becomes active at all the various sources of libidinal pleasure" (Klein 1930, p. 219).

39. Klein does not explain further why this should be the case. What follows is consequently an attempt at a reconstruction that we cannot merely base on her texts.

40. Here it is evident that Klein adopts Freud's narrow definition of self-preservation. Self-preservation and vital survival primarily refer to hunger and thirst. Klein writes, for example, that the feelings of the child in the first instance refer to the "feeding relationship with the mother" (Klein 1952, p. 64) as if the child would only and primarily have to be fed. We will discuss the untenable nature of this point of view further. To hold to this view makes it impossible to ascribe to the problematic of attachment the proper place it is due.

41. Klein herself is here indeed mainly concerned with the manner in which the biological death instinct is directed outward.

THE POSITIONS OF THE SUBJECT

Klein links the different defense mechanisms against anxiety with two subjective positions—the paranoid-schizoid and depressive positions—each of which is characterized by a specific experience of the self and a specific experience of reality. She defines each of these two positions as a systematic connection of defense mechanisms that are characteristic for a certain period of the development of the young child. She further describes these normal defense mechanisms in light of the pathologies that they help elucidate. In the paranoid-schizoid position, the processes of splitting, disavowal, and idealization mainly come to the fore. This position characterizes the first two to three months of life. It is dominated by the anxiety of destruction of one's own ego, whereas the objects to which the subject relates are still of a partial nature. The development of the perceptual capacities and the cognitive functions make it after some time possible for the child to relate to a total object—paradigmatically, the mother—and to enter into an affective and significant bond with it. The nature of anxiety also changes through this process. It is no longer the anxiety of being destroyed that is all-determinative, but rather the anxiety of damaging the loved object by one's own aggressivity (and thereby endangering one's own continued existence). From now on, depressive feelings and the attempts to (phantasmatically) repair the damage are central.

Does this also mean that every child, according to Klein, goes through periods that we must define as schizophrenic or depressive in the psychiatric sense of the terms? Klein explicitly denies this. On the contrary, she speaks of positions in order to avoid this confusion. In the first instance, writes Klein, it is better to speak of positions rather than phases of development, because neither of these ever becomes exclusively dominant in normal development. The development of the child cannot exclusively be understood from the point of view of paranoid-schizoid and depressive anxieties and defense mechanisms (Klein 1935). There is more in the world of the child than can be described in terms of these anxieties and defense mechanisms.[42] Furthermore, pathology must not be explained as a mere repetition of, or regression to, one of these two positions. Depression in the clinical sense of the term, for example, is not simply a regression to the depressive position. On the contrary, according to Klein, clinical depression presupposes a reactivation of the paranoid-schizoid position, without which it cannot be understood. Klein (1935) also points out that childhood is characterized by the rapidly changing transition from the paranoid-schizoid position to the depressive position and vice versa. Such flexibility is lacking in (adult) pathology. Finally and most importantly, the forces that will permit overcoming the anxieties and defense mechanisms by which they are characterized are in principle already at work in the paranoid-schizoid and depressive positions (Klein 1952). The latter is not the case with pathology in the strict sense of the term, according to Klein. In other words, Klein understands and defines subjectivity in light of anxieties and mechanisms that refer to the (possibility of) pathology in an intrinsic fashion, but to which, at the same time, it cannot simply be reduced.[43]

According to Klein, the defense mechanisms that play a decisive role in both of these positions have a phantasmatic character. The processes of splitting hence do not refer to the actual state of affairs, but rather to the way in which the young child experiences and orders these.

---

42. However, Klein never explored this problematic further. It is evident that this would be the point at which she could have discovered attachment as an autonomous dimension of human existence. Klein (1935) writes, for example, that a good relation to the mother and to the external reality is a condition for the overcoming of the earliest paranoid anxieties. Elsewhere she explicitly links this problematic with the theory of attachment (Klein 1952). In this respect, however, Klein never gets any further than suggestions that she does not develop. The reason for this is that undoubtedly Klein is not able first to understand relations to the object as a defense against primitive anxiety, and then to understand attachment as an independent and autonomous problematic, not based on anything else.

43. In an analogous fashion, Freud, for example, defines the infantile instincts in light of the perversions, which does not mean that the infant may be called perverse in the clinical sense of the term. The child, however, does carry the intrinsic possibility of this derailment within him- or herself.

Analogously, the depressive anxieties that the love object might be damaged in most cases do not coincide with actual damage to this object. The latter only takes place in the experience and phantasy of the child. Klein's positions consequently refer to the way in which reality is deformed and experienced by the young child in a never-ending attempt to master its anxieties.

The paranoid-schizoid and the depressive position have a genetic as well as a structural significance. They refer to structuring moments of subjectivity. Klein indeed emphasizes that these mechanisms play a lasting role in our relation to reality. On the one hand, Klein continually gives the impression that psychic development is aimed at a progressive integration of the ego, which must relate to reality in a realistic fashion—that is to say, a fashion not skewed by phantasies. In the paranoid-schizoid position, the early ego is still scarcely integrated and is dominated by the mechanism of splitting, which still further endangers its cohesion. Under the influence of the life instincts, the ego indeed attempts from the beginning of its existence to overcome this tendency to fragmentation. In this process of progressive integration, the depressive position plays a decisive role. On the other hand, Klein also stresses that during our entire existence both positions remain active with alternating intensity. A complete overcoming of either the paranoid-schizoid or the depressive anxieties is not possible. Normality can only be described as a precarious and changeable equilibrium between these two potentially pathological positions (Klein 1963).

First we shall attempt to define the paranoid-schizoid and the depressive positions in more detail.[44] Subsequently we will address the status of phantasy in Klein's work more in depth.

---

44. We do not wish to provide an exhaustive discussion of the Kleinian position in what follows. We limit ourselves to what is necessary for the development of our problematic. In so doing, we will attempt as far as possible to reconstruct the mechanisms that Klein describes in an objectivizing and concretizing manner, from the perspective of the corporeal experiences that provide their basis.

The Paranoid-Schizoid Position

Klein tells the story of a little boy who had the habit of pretending that he was in possession of all kinds of wild animals, such as elephants, leopards, wolves, and hyenas. According to Klein, these animals represented dangerous objects that persecuted the child. The child, however, had succeeded in taming these animals and in making them instrumental in his own defense against any number of enemies. Klein continues that in the analysis it appeared that these animals also represented the boy's own sadism and that each animal indicated a specific corporeal source of this sadism. The elephants, for example, represented the sadism that had its origin in the muscles and the impulses of the child to kick and stomp. The leopards represented his teeth and nails and their function in his own attacks. The wolves referred to the excrements of the child and their destructive properties.[45] Sometimes, however, the little boy was afraid that these animals would turn against him and kill him. Klein says that in this way he expresses his own anxiety of his own destructive impulses, which he had projected onto these animals. It is noteworthy that Klein mainly emphasizes the anxiety of the little boy of being destroyed by his own destructive impulses, on the one hand, and the way in which the child defends himself against this anxiety on the other hand. This problematic characterizes the paranoid-schizoid position and must be traced back and linked to the mechanisms available to the young child to defend against the most archaic anxieties of destruction. What are these mechanisms and how do they determine the primitive experience of the self and of reality?

How does external reality receive meaning for the young child, and how does the child relate to it? In several places in his work, Freud describes how, under the influence of the pleasure principle, children take into themselves all "good" objects (introjection) and eject all unpleasurable

---

45. In this context, one should remember what we have said in the above discussion about erogenous zones as the source of aggressive impulses.

objects (projection). The early ego is confronted with external reality for the first time by the vital needs. Since the sexual instinct is initially auto-erotic, only the instinct of self-preservation requires, according to Freud, an external object in order to be satisfied. The satisfaction of vital needs, however, does not prevent the infant from regularly experiencing inner unpleasure. Freud writes that under the influence of the pleasure principle a further evolution occurs. Infants take the objects that they experience as pleasurable into themselves and reject the objects that they experience as unpleasurable. In this way the original "*real-ich*" is replaced by a purified pleasure-ego. Infants want to ban all unpleasure from within themselves and hence project all unpleasure into the external world, which thereby receives a hostile character (Freud 1915a). In the language of the oral instinct: "This I wish to eat (because it is pleasurable); this I wish to spit out (because it causes unpleasure)."

Klein agrees with Freud that the original relation to reality must be understood on the basis of the mechanisms of introjection and projection. According to Klein (1946), these mechanisms from the outset have a defensive significance. Klein assumes that young children immediately experience any inner unpleasure as an attack on their ego, against which they must defend themselves. The ego does so by evacuating what is bad to the outside or by projecting it outside.[46] The introjection of the "good" object is also a defense against anxiety. By taking the good object into itself and identifying with it, the ego protects itself against the anxiety of being destroyed by the bad object in itself as well as outside itself.[47]

---

46. We speak of "evacuation or projection" because the most archaic forms of projection must be thought on the basis of the model of, for example, vomiting. The basic psychic mechanisms all have their primal model in corporeal activities. According to Klein, children who vomit immediately experience this as a spitting out of what they experience as bad in themselves (Rivière 1936).

47. Traditionally, psychoanalysis considers incorporation to be the precursor to identification. Primitive forms of introjection must also be understood on the basis of archaic corporeal experiences. We might perhaps present this as follows: The young child who is being fed and feels satisfied, as it were, completely coincides with this experience of satisfaction. The experience of satisfaction does not yet refer to its future absence. We shall return to this point presently.

According to Klein, these mechanisms primarily refer to partial objects and in particular the breast.[48] It would be wrong, however, to interpret this too literally. The breast, after all, refers to the various positive (pleasurable) and negative (unpleasurable) experiences children have in their relationship with their mother (or whoever replaces her). The breast consequently is a metaphor that also refers to the way in which the mother holds and cuddles the child or to the sound of her voice (Klein 1952, 1964, Rivière 1936). According to Klein, in the first instance the mother is not yet comprehended as a unity and totality. Children do not yet experience the pleasurable and unpleasurable aspects of the mother as aspects of one and the same person. They do not yet associate the first pleasurable and unpleasurable experience as linked with one and the same object in which they originate. This means that the primitive experiences of pleasure and unpleasure are initially experienced as more or less mutually independent. The relative weakness of the as yet scarcely integrated ego results in the infant not being able to relate these experiences to one another and to connect them with one another so that they would be part of one and the same history. This lack of integration of the ego corresponds to a weakly integrated experience of reality.

In this way it becomes comprehensible how and why splitting can play such a central role in the first months of life. By splitting, Klein understands the psychical mechanism on the basis of which the young child tries to keep the good and bad breasts apart as far as possible. Something is bad or good but never a little of each. This mechanism relates closely to introjection and projection and is further supported by the poor integration of the ego that is in turn reinforced by it. We recall that young children direct the aggressivity by which they are threatened of the ego from within onto an external (proto)object (from which they are then anxious of being attacked). At the same time they are being satisfied at regular intervals. These experiences of satisfaction, according to Klein, are experienced as victories over the bad breast, which can thus be kept at a distance.

---

48. This, by the way, also holds with Freud. He too assumes that the initial pleasure ego only relates to partial objects.

The child is simply its own bliss, and so the child feels safe against the attacks of the bad breast. This feeling of security and well-being is reinforced further by the fact that pleasure and unpleasure are initially experienced as being more or less mutually independent. The experience of satisfaction does not yet anticipate its future disappearance.

According to Klein, the good and bad breasts are not only experienced as more or less separate states factually. She claims that the child also pursues this split actively. Children attempt to protect the good breast, which they love, against the bad breast, which they hate and from which they fear aggressivity. They attempt to keep the good breast completely out of reach of the bad breast. According to Klein (1946), the mechanisms of idealization and hallucinatory wish-fulfillment help the child to accomplish this task. In the "Project for a Scientific Psychology", Freud (1895/1962) writes that when the infant is hungry he is able to make the object that would still his hunger present to himself by means of a hallucination.[49] In this way the infant is able to bear his frustrations for a little while. Put in a more Kleinian language, this means that in so doing, the infant is able to maintain the split between the good and the bad breast (Rivière 1936). In other words, the mechanism of splitting is an extension of the fragmented and fragmentary experience of reality that it at the same time reinforces and that characterizes the first months of life.[50]

Klein (1946) further links this possibility to the power of instinctual life, which aims at unlimited satisfaction. In young children, the reality test is indeed not yet, or is only hardly, developed. Consequently, they cannot yet measure the demands of their instincts against real possibilities for satisfaction. External reality does not yet offer resistance to their wishes so that they may believe that wishing something and getting it are one and the same thing. The great and compelling force of the instinct combined with the absence, or incomplete devel-

---

49. For a more extensive commentary, see Van Haute and Geyskens 2004.

50. "In the discussion following the reading of this paper, Dr. W. C. M. Scott referred to another aspect of splitting. He stressed the importance of the breaks in continuity of experience, which imply a splitting in time rather than in space" (Klein 1946, p. 6).

opment, of a concept of reality leads to the conviction that what is strived for is also actually realized. The young child who spits out what is bad in it and experiences this activity as an attack immediately equates this attack with the destruction of the object.

The idealization of the good breast contributes to the splitting and to the destruction of the bad object. The infant, writes Klein (1946), exaggerates the good aspects of the breast in order to protect itself against the bad breast. We might perhaps best imagine this idealization as follows. The young child who is satisfied "forgets" not only the state of unpleasure that has just been alleviated, but at the same time has a tendency to absolutize this new state. In the experience of children the newly acquired well-being is not disturbed or threatened by anything. It is a state without lack, in which they know themselves to be unquestionably safe against the attacks of the bad breast, the existence of which is disavowed. They now experience themselves as simply goodness, from which any anxiety, and any aggressivity against that which had caused anxiety, are excluded. Klein concludes, "The omnipotent denial of the existence of the bad object and of the painful situation is the unconscious equal to annihilation by the destructive impulse. It is, however, not only a situation and an object that are denied and annihilated—*it is an object-relation* which suffers this fate; and therefore a part of the ego from which the feelings towards the object emanate, is denied and annihilated as well" (Klein 1946, p. 7, her italics). The denial of psychic reality—that is to say, of the intrinsic interwovenness of the good and the bad, of aggressivity and love, in me as well as outside of me—is an essential part of the paranoid-schizoid position.

In earliest childhood, the oral zone and oral instincts play a decisive role, according to Klein. And yet, other libidinous and aggressive impulses and phantasies, which have their origins in other erogenous zones, come to the fore fairly quickly. Oral, urethral, and anal instincts of an aggressive as well as of a libidinous nature, in their mutual relation, determine the relation of the infant to him- or herself and to reality. According to Klein, in the paranoid-schizoid position this relation is characterized by a specific dramatic dynamic in which the mechanisms described play the main part.[51] Klein, for example, describes how the body of the mother is experienced as an extension of the breast before the child is yet able to grasp her as a unity and totality. The aggressivity of the child can now turn against the body of the mother, which the child wishes to deprive of all its good contents. The child wants to be satisfied and the absence of satisfaction evokes its aggressivity. In children's experience it will be as if they literally suck the mother dry and remove all good objects from her. But the aggressivity toward, as well as love for, the mother can also occur along other paths. For example, the expulsion of excrements can be experienced as the projection of dangerous objects out of the self into the mother.[52] Together with these bad objects, bad (aggressive) parts of the self are placed in the object. As with the omnipotent destruction of the object, here too we are dealing with an object relation and not only with an object. The hate and the aggressivity children sensed in their own selves now appear to emanate from the object, which becomes a persecutor.[53] This may have as a consequence that introjection is from now on experienced as an intrusion of the external world into the self. According to Klein, one may see this dynamic at work in certain psychotic scenarios, and more particularly in paranoia, in which the subject has the sensation that the external world has taken possession of it (knows his thoughts and so on).

---

51. Our exposition does indeed make clear that the various mechanisms that characterize the paranoid-schizoid position can only be adequately understood in their mutual interconnectedness.

52. We cannot stress enough that we are dealing here with the description of very basic and in particular corporeal processes and mechanisms in the language of adults. That which we describe here can be reconstructed as follows: the pain that the child experiences during excretion immediately qualifies the object as bad and the activity by which it is expelled as an attack. Under no circumstances may we ascribe conceptual content to this experience. The child does not yet form for itself a representation of what it does—as yet there are no mental objects in the proper sense—but it immediately gives a subjective interpretation to what it experiences in the depth of its body (Klein 1946, Rivière 1936).

53. In this context, Klein speaks of projective identification. Laplanche and Pontalis (1967) define this projective identification as follows: "[A] term introduced by Melanie Klein: a mechanism revealed in phantasies in which the subject inserts his self—in whole or in part—into the object, in order to harm, possess, or control it" (p. 356).

Not only the bad parts of the self are expelled but also the good (lovable) aspects thereof. The feces may also be experienced as gifts to the object that satisfies and protects the child (Klein 1946). They are projected into, and are thus experienced as part of, the object that the child loves because he or she is satisfied by it. Klein points out that the projection of good parts of the self into the object permits the child to develop a good object relation with the mother and to integrate its ego. The development of the ego indeed presupposes that the young child is able to experience the mother as being fundamentally good, supportive, and helpful. According to Klein, the projection of one's own good objects adds to this.

The effect of introjection is equally important for the development of object relations. The introjection of the good breast that represents the life instinct is a condition of possibility for a balanced development (Klein 1948). We should probably conceive of this as follows. Children who receive the breast or are being fed have the feeling that they take the good object into themselves and that they in a certain sense become one with it. The experience of containing the good, of having it within oneself, and of coinciding with it, according to Klein, forms the core of the ego and contributes to its cohesion. After all, it protects the ego against the feeling of being pursued from within by the bad object and from having to protect oneself by splitting and projection. The child experiences the introjected good object as the origin of life that must be protected at all costs (Klein 1948).[54]

Along with the breast, the feces, and the urine, Klein also refers to the penis as an important object in the original paranoid-schizoid position.[55] Here, too, it would be wrong to understand Klein's reference to the penis too visually. On the contrary, Klein presupposes that

---

54. According to Klein, the introjected good and bad breasts together constitute the core of the superego. We will return to this point in the discussion on sexuality in the work of Klein.

55. As such it may already be evident that Klein situates the first beginnings of the oedipal problematic, including the formation of the superego, in earliest infancy. At the same time, the reference to the penis also indicates that the frequently aired critique that Klein does not know the father must at the least be nuanced.

the young child already has a certain intuitive understanding[56] of the presence of a third—prototypically, and in the language of the adult, the father—who possesses something that the mother desires or needs. If the mother desires this something, then it must be good. According to Klein, children interpret this good automatically in the language of their own corporeality, in which oral instincts still play the main role. This is why Klein may speak about the "feeding" penis. Conversely, the penis of the father may also be experienced as a threat to one's own satisfaction; when the mother doesn't come to help quickly enough, this may be because something that she finds more important holds her back. The penis thereby receives a threatening and hostile character. According to Klein, the child also interprets this threat according to its own body language. That which threatens me and has hostile intentions toward me can bite me and tear me up—which is also to say, bite and tear up the good breast that feeds me.[57]

The problematic of the paranoid-schizoid position, according to Klein, belongs to being human as such. No one escapes from it. At the same time, the vicissitudes of the instincts of this position constitute the basis for later psychotic pathologies. The way in which we succeed in dealing with our aggressivity and the anxieties connected thereto in our earliest childhood determines our further course of life. When, for example, aggressivity is too strong, introjection of the good object may also be experienced as being destructive. According to Klein, children have corporeal knowledge of the fact that the consumption of the object immediately implies, or may imply, its destruction (Isaacs 1948).[58] In this manner infants may have the feeling that they have ruined the

---

56. This understanding is itself corporeal. In their daily contact with the mother, young children experience that something else is at play. The mother places the child into the arms of the father because she has more urgent preoccupations, and so forth.

57. Klein also adds that the young child can have the feeling that the penis of the father is situated in the mother. The child also interprets the relation of the mother to the penis in oral terms, such that the child may introject it together with the breast. We would, however, stray too far, if we were to elaborate this problematic in any detail.

58. We will return to this point more extensively in the discussion on the significance of phantasy in Klein's work.

good breast, and that the latter is now attacking them from within, coercing the children to defend themselves against the anxiety of persecution in an excessive fashion.[59] Excessive splitting of object relations, for example, may lead to the young child having the feeling of falling apart and of no longer being a unit. Further development may in this way be seriously compromised.

After a few months the cognitive, perceptive, and affective capacities of the child, according to Klein, have developed sufficiently to permit the recognition of the object in its totality and unity.[60] This implies an important change in the relation to self and to the surrounding reality. The paranoid-schizoid position is gradually replaced by the depressive position, in which anxiety about having damaged the object, not the anxiety of destruction, is central. Feelings of guilt and the attempt to repair the damage are the consequence.[61]

The Depressive Position

Klein writes that the depressive position comes on the scene in the fourth month of life when the infant has become able to introject the entire object—prototypically the mother (Klein 1946). It is evident that in this case we are not dealing with a bodily incorporation of an object, as was the case in the preceding period. This statement indeed only makes sense when it addresses a (visual) memory image to which the

---

59. According to Klein, the good breast is codeterminative for early eating disorders (Klein 1948).

60. It is self-evident that the introduction of the depressive position is not solely dependent on cognitive and perceptual development. In this context, Klein especially emphasizes the importance of the introjection of a good, loving object, which creates a feeling of well-being. When young children have the feeling that they carry the good internal object in themselves, they are much stronger and have much more self-confidence when coming under stress (see also Hinshelwood 1994).

61. However, this does not mean that paranoid-schizoid defense mechanisms are entirely overcome. It only means that they do not continue to exercise an all-conquering role in which the experience of the child remains dominated by an excessive anxiety of being destroyed.

child is attached and that the child cherishes. The love object is internalized so that the infant may, for example, when he or she is lonely, recall this image in order to lessen the pain without immediately having to take recourse to paranoid-schizoid mechanisms.

In the paranoid-schizoid position, meaning is still stuck to corporeal experience as such. There is not yet a real distinction between stimuli, sensation, and significance. There are not yet mental objects in the proper sense. This changes in the depressive position. The change goes hand in hand with the development of visual capacities, which progressively come to provide the measure of the child's relation to him- or herself and to others. For this very reason, the child is now able to construct mental objects that he or she can incorporate in a manner that is not merely corporeal.[62] Also, in experience a progressive distinction between what belongs to the body as such and what may be called psychic begins to emerge.

The institution of the primacy of the visual also means that the child is able to form a total image of the mother. This is much more difficult as long as children primarily relate to their environment by means of tactile or olfactory perceptions. The senses of touch and smell reveal much less about the aspect of totality of an object than visual perception does. We always feel only a very limited part of an object from which we can take no distance in tactile sensation. Visual perception, by contrast, forces us to take a distance from the object that now stands before us and allows us—in any case frontally—to perceive the object in its totality. According to Klein (1946), the latter also allows for a more adequate perception of, and adaptation to, reality.[63]

---

62. Making use of more contemporary language, we might also say that from now on the child is able to "mentalize."

63. Thus, it also becomes clear why Lacan (1949) links the depressive position to what he calls the mirror stage. After all, the mirror stage is the moment in which the child identifies with the image of its body as a totality for the first time and in which, according to Lacan, the ego comes into existence. From this moment onward the child is able to relate to objects in their totality. Like the depressive position, the mirror stage therefore also implies a primacy of the visual. Yet there are also important differences between the depressive position and the mirror stage. According to Lacan, what is primary is not the relation to the mother, but the relation to one's own mirror image.

Together with the perception of the object in its totality comes the realization that the same object is responsible for the satisfaction of needs and its absence. The loved and hated aspects of the mother can no longer be separated from one another in the same way as in the paranoid-schizoid position.[64] On the contrary, feelings of love and hate are from now on experienced in relation to one and the same object. This results in the increased anxiety of the loss of the love object, and in particular in the anxiety that this loss is to be ascribed to one's own aggressive impulses. This explains the great importance of feelings of guilt in this position. Children feel guilty about the damage they cause the love object and attempt to repair that damage. According to Klein (1946), feelings of guilt and states similar to that of mourning in adults form the affective core of the depressive position. The latter also indicates an increased recognition of psychic reality: bad objects and one's own aggressive tendencies are no longer simply ignored, but are experienced in their intrinsic conflict with loving tendencies. In what follows we shall attempt further to elucidate the problematic of the depressive position by means of two clinical examples, which will also help us to define the relation between the paranoid-schizoid position and the depressive position more closely.[65]

The dialectic between mother and child, as described by Klein, only becomes possible, according to Lacan, on the basis of the identification with one's own mirror image. In this sense, Lacan also reinterprets the paranoid-schizoid position from the standpoint of the primacy of the visual and as a *nachträglich* effect of the mirror stage (Lacan 1949, 1975; for further commentary see Van Haute 2005). Finally, for Klein there can be no talk of the ego only coming into existence in the depressive position. On the contrary, according to her the ego is present from the very beginning onward. A detailed comparison of Klein's depressive position and Lacan's mirror stage would lead us too far astray here.

64. In later texts, however, Klein writes that such ambivalent relations are already possible toward partial objects. The distinction between the paranoid-schizoid and the depressive position is thus disconnected from the distinction between partial and total objects.

65. For what is to follow, see Klein 1935.

Further Reflections on the Paranoid-Schizoid Position and the Depressive Position

Klein tells of an adult patient who suffered from severe hypochondriac and paranoid anxieties. As a child he was told that he had a tapeworm. In analysis the patient linked the worm to his greed. At the same time he had the sensation that the worm was making its way through his body and he developed a great anxiety of getting cancer. Toward Klein he was extremely suspicious. He feared that she conspired with the people who did not mean him well. During this period he dreamt of a detective who arrested a hostile person and put him into prison. However, the detective also did not appear to be trustworthy. In fact, he was in league with the enemy. From the associations of this patient it became apparent that the detective represented his analyst—Klein. Klein adds that the patient had internalized this situation of anxiety and that it was linked to his phantasy concerning tapeworms. The prison was his own body, and it became evident, Klein reports, that the tapeworm represented his two parents united in a hostile coalition—united in coitus, writes Klein—against him.[66] How are we to understand this?

In the stories and anxieties of her patient, Klein recognizes the psychotic anxieties and mechanisms that are predominant in the first months of life. The phantasy and the anxiety about having cancer refer to the bad objects that the patient senses within himself in a concrete corporeal manner—just as in the original paranoid-schizoid position—and that he feels attack him from within. To this hostile internal world corresponds an external hostile reality. The external reality is peopled by persons who wish to cause the patient harm. Ultimately these persons refer to the bad parents of the patient. That Klein in this context speaks of the parents during coitus is merely the translation into the language of the adult—and of the somewhat older child—of the feeling of being denied access to the

---

66. Among other things, Klein deduced this from the fact that tapeworms, according to the patient, were bisexual. The phantasy of the combined parental figures is, according to Klein, characteristic of the earliest stages of the Oedipus complex.

intimacy of the parents.[67] Whatever the case may be, according to the logic of the paranoid-schizoid position the objects are taken up into a permanent dynamics of introjection and projection that is experienced in the body itself. The bad detective/analyst, for example, is linked to the phantasy of the tapeworm that eats the patient from within. The mechanism of splitting is also prominently present: the detective first takes the side of the analysand, but then quickly becomes his enemy. He is either the one or the other.

Klein assumes that these mechanisms and anxieties are reactivated by the current situation of the patient. We could, for example, think here of a disappointment at work or in one's love life.[68] In other words, in the associations of her patient Klein discovers the deferred actions of mechanisms of defense that had dominated the life of the baby.[69] The current problematic of Klein's patient is determined by the way in which he lived through the paranoid-schizoid and depressive position as an infant. Here we may identify the Freudian mechanism of *Nachträglichkeit* (deferred action).[70] Freud primarily introduces this concept in connection with his seduction theory of neurosis. It implies that the memory of trauma has an effect on the psyche only in a second instance—namely at the begin-

---

67. We may easily imagine that during the course of his analysis the patient did express this feeling in such words. The child does indeed link the feeling of not gaining access to the world of the parents to their sexual relationship fairly quickly. Klein (1935) writes that the patient, for example, attempted to disturb the parents during sex by relieving himself at that moment. She interprets this as aggressivity against the— literally interwoven—parents and speaks of the phantasy of "combined parents." Yet it is obviously only much later that these experiences and feelings can be grasped and formulated in terms of coitus and sexuality in the strict sense.

68. In this case study Klein does not provide any further information on the point. However, since the patient did not suffer from paranoid anxieties all his life, it is safe to assume that something in his circumstances must have led to the reactivation of paranoid-schizoid mechanisms

69. This implies that interpretation in Kleinian analysis primarily refers to the infantile mechanisms and not infantile contents that are addressed in free association. Developing this problematic further would be beyond the scope of this chapter.

70. For a discussion of the concept of *Nachträglichkeit* in Freud's work, see Laplanche 1992; we will return to this point extensively in Chapter 3 when discussing the difference between the psychoanalytic concept of time and the concept of time in the theory of attachment.

ning of puberty.[71] In his later theory of sexuality this concept means that the original infantile experiences of pleasure only receive a problematic character after the advent of "organic repression," and the reaction formations of guilt, shame, and morality.[72] Analogously the paranoid-schizoid mechanisms are reactivated in a second instance by the current problematic of the patient, according to Klein.[73] At the same time these mechanisms are now expressed in the language of the adult or of the older child. That which was first sensed in the immediate corporeal experience of the infant is now put into words and subsumed into the language of the psychotic subject.

Let us briefly return to Klein's case study of the man who was being eaten by worms. Klein (1935) writes: "While the paranoid anxieties predominated and the anxiety of his bad united objects prevailed, X felt only hypochondriacal anxieties for his own body. When depression and sorrow had set in, the love and the concern for the good object came to the fore and the anxiety-contents as well as the whole feelings and defenses altered" (p. 274). In analysis, a turn from anxiety to concern has occurred. This turn coincides with the advent of the depressive position. Klein (1935) talks, for example, of another patient who suffered from paranoid and hypochondriac complaints. He talked every day for hours about bodily discomforts for which he held other people in his surroundings responsible. When during the course of his analysis his suspicion decreases, his relation to Klein also improves. It becomes apparent that concealed behind his accu-

---

71. That is to say, at the moment that the child is able to really grasp the sexual significance of the trauma. (For further commentary on Freud's theory of seduction, see Van Haute and Geyskens 2004.)

72. See Infantile Amnesia and Organic Repression in Chapter 1; also see Geyskens 2003.

73. Nevertheless, there is an important difference between Freud and Klein with regard to the theory of *Nachträglichkeit*. In Freud's work, *Nachträglichkeit* principally refers to psychic content that in the first instance has no effect, nor does it have or can it have a problematic character. With Klein on the other hand, it refers to positions that in and of themselves already have a psychic effectiveness and that can give rise to all kinds of problems. We shall return to this point in Chapter 3.

sations of others is a deep love for his mother and great concern for his parents. This discovery is accompanied by deep depression. During this period the hypochondriac complaints also change with regard to the way in which they are presented in the analysis, as well as with regard to the psychic content that they can be associated with. In truth, the patient continues to complain about bodily discomforts, but immediately begins to talk about which medication he has taken for his throat, his bowels, and so on. It was, writes Klein, as if he was taking care of his sick organs and body parts. At the same time the patient, a teacher, talked about his concern for the young people entrusted to his care, as well as for some members of his family. According to Klein, it quickly became apparent that this patient identified the organs and body parts that he cared for with his internalized brothers and sisters, toward whom he felt guilty and whom he tried to keep alive in this way. The hypochondriac complaints were therefore no longer exclusively experienced in relation to the ego that felt threatened by them, such as is the case in the paranoid-schizoid position, but they now also acquired a relation to the objects the patient had internalized. In his phantasies his family members had fallen victim to his own aggressivity against which he also had to protect them.

In contrast to the paranoid-schizoid position, mutually opposed affects—love, concern, and hate—are here experienced with regard to the same object. The excessive anxiety of this patient of the consequences of his aggressivity toward his love objects and his subsequent concern and desperation are, according to Klein (1935), precisely the reasons that lead to an intensification of paranoid anxieties and defense mechanisms. The subject had identified with the damaged object and consequently protested against the suffering to which it now fell prey. From that moment on all attention went to the state of the self—the paranoid and hypochondriac complaints—and the object disappeared from view. On the basis of the identification with the loved and yet threatened object, the anxiety about one's own existence characteristic for the paranoid-schizoid position regained the upper hand. Consequently, the reactivation of paranoid-schizoid mechanisms of defense followed. Love and concern for the other as well as identification therewith are for the moment pushed out of view by hate.[74]

Klein's case study once again illustrates the concept of deferred action (*Nachträglichkeit*) to which we have already referred. Paranoid anxieties are reactivated from a depressive problematic and the way in which it is experienced by the patient. From that moment onward, the depressive problematic is overshadowed and eclipsed by the deferred effect of the paranoid-schizoid mechanisms of defense. Psychoanalytic time is therefore not merely linear, but also a time in which previous moments and mechanisms may reemerge into the foreground because of later events and problems.

Phantasy in the Work of Klein

We have already pointed out that the paranoid-schizoid and the depressive mechanisms of defense have a phantasmatic character. Since both positions already occur in early childhood, this also means that according to Klein phantasies must already be present immediately after birth. But how are we to understand these phantasies of early childhood, and how are they related to what Freud and the psychoanalytic tradition understand by the concept of phantasy? Freud understands phantasy[75] as an imaginary scenario in which the subject may or may not be explicitly present as an agent, and which represents the realization of a sexual and object-related desire (conscious or not) in a distorted manner.[76]

---

74. Klein's idea that depression in the clinical sense should not exclusively be understood on the basis of the depressive position also plays a role here in the background. She writes: "I must again make clear that in my view the depressive state is based on the paranoid state and genetically derived from it. I consider the depressive state as being the result of a mixture of paranoid anxiety and of those anxiety contents, distressed feelings and defenses which are connected with the impending loss of the whole loved object" (Klein 1935, p. 275).

75. For a definition of Freudian phantasy see Laplanche and Pontalis 1967.

76. This distortion occurs on the basis of the defense mechanisms that play a role in the formation of phantasy. Like the symptom, phantasy is a compromise between (unconscious) desires and higher psychic processes to which these desires are unacceptable.

Although phantasies may sometimes be described in one sentence,[77] we are always dealing with articulated scenes which may in principle be represented in a visual fashion and dramatized.[78]

In his texts up until 1910, Freud wrote that phantasies only begin to play a role in psychic life from puberty onward. After all, infantile sexuality, in contrast to adult sexuality, is essentially autoerotic and objectless. Infantile sexuality does not require an object apart from one's own body. Sexual instincts are during infancy still satisfied in and on the body itself, and are not yet related to an object in the external world (Freud 1905b).[79] For Freud this implies that the infantile instinctual life is not mediated by phantasies, for phantasies always involve a relation (albeit perhaps minimal) to an object that is not the body itself. In his texts from 1910 onward, Freud stresses the similarity between infant and adult sexuality more and more. Indeed, as a consequence of the introduction of the Oedipus complex, infantile sexuality becomes also intrinsically related to external objects. Freud now writes that the object choice that he had thought to be characteristic for puberty occurs much earlier—more precisely between the second and third year of life (Freud 1905b). This means that already from a very early age on—during the oedipal phase—the child aims its sexual instinct toward a person of the other sex.[80] From this per-

---

77. One may, for example, think of Freud's (1919) analysis of the eponymous phantasy from *A Child Is Being Beaten*.

78. This is also the case for Lacanian phantasy. Lacan understands phantasy as a scenario of signifiers from which the subject, which does not coincide with any signifier, nevertheless derives some consistency. In this way the subject receives a determination that differs from the determination that it acquires through an identification with an imaginary (and hence by definition visual) gestalt. However, this does not mean that the Lacanian phantasy doesn't primarily reveal itself as a scene with visual characteristics that haunts the analysand. According to Lacan, however, the imaginary characteristics of phantasy do not constitute its essence, but must rather be understood as the "imaginarization" of the signifiers that determine its structure and content. (For further commentary on phantasy in the work of Lacan, see Dekesel 2002, Schokker and Schokker 2000, Van Haute 2002.)

79. For further commentary see Van Haute and Geyskens 2004. We shall return to this problematic in the following chapter.

spective, Freud can also ascribe a phantasmatic character to infantile sexuality. However, Freud continues to think that the genesis of phantasy coincides with the beginning of the Oedipus complex or with the first expression of object-related sexuality. This is also the period in which the child begins to develop its first "infantile theories of sexuality" about the question of where children come from and about sexual difference. These infantile sexual theories are the earliest phantasmatic activities of the child.

Before the age of two or three years, however, according to Freud, there is no phantasmatic activity in the child. Klein, on the contrary, calls the paranoid-schizoid mechanisms of defense "phantasmatic," which implies that she allows for phantasmatic activity to commence much earlier—properly speaking, practically from birth. Can the concept of phantasy signify the same in a child of two or three years of age—and *a fortiori* in the adult—as in the newborn? Must we not redefine phantasy in order to be able to use it in the way in which Klein does? We are here in fact confronted with a problematic that is analogous to the introduction of infantile sexuality in Freud's work. Freud not only extends sexuality into childhood. This extension is only possible if we redefine sexuality. With Klein we may identify a similar move: The extension of phantasmatic activity into the earliest infancy, immediately compels her to redefine its meaning. The phantasies of the paranoid-schizoid position differ radically from those of the depressive position and *a fortiori* from the phantasies of the adult. What does this mean?[81]

---

80. And yet here too an important difference between infantile and adult sexuality remains: according to Freud the young child interprets sexual difference as a function of the presence or absence of the male organ. For commentary on this problematic, see Van Haute and Geyskens 2004.

81. Klein wrote relatively little on the status of phantasy. In the context of the discussion between Anna Freud and Melanie Klein and her followers, which tore the British Psycho-Analytical Society apart in the 1940s, Susan Isaacs, one of Klein's more gifted followers, wrote a brilliant article on phantasy in the work of Klein. She wrote the text in close collaboration with Klein, who cites it in agreement in several points in her own work (Klein 1959). We therefore feel justified in reading Klein's concept of phantasy in light of Isaacs's text (in this context also see Rivière 1952). For an

According to Klein, phantasies constitute the primary and proper content of the unconscious. They are the psychic representatives of the instinct. Or better, and more precisely: by means of phantasy the instinct receives a psychic existence (Klein 1959). All instincts, all feelings, all mechanisms of defense are expressed in phantasies that determine their sense and direction. Consequently phantasies cannot, according to Klein, be thought of exclusively in terms of hallucinatory wish fulfillment. Most phantasies also serve other goals than mere instinctual satisfaction. On the contrary, they are, for example, in the service of disavowal, of reparation, or of the omnipotent control of the object (Isaacs 1948).

Klein emphasizes again and again that in principle these phantasies are preverbal (Isaacs 1948). However, we cannot investigate phantasy without converting it into words. Yet this "translation" of phantasy implies that we add an element alien to it that belongs to the later stages of psychic development.[82] Isaacs (1948) writes, for example, about an 18-month-old girl who cries out in anxiety at the sight of her mother's shoe, the sole of which has become detached. For a whole week, she cringed every time she saw her mother going about wearing the shoe. Indeed the mother could only avoid terrorizing the infant by wearing brightly colored slippers. The anxiety attacks came to an end only when the mother stopped wearing the dreaded shoe. More than a year later, the child suddenly asked: "Where are your broken shoes?" and adds, "They might have eaten me right up!" The child, Isaacs concludes, saw the shoe as an open mouth and reacted accordingly, even if she could not express the same in language at that very moment.[83]

---

exhaustive overview of the discussion between Anna Freudians and Kleinians in the British Psycho-Analytical Society, see King and Steiner 1991.

82. Isaacs also points out that adult phantasy escapes the "logic and systematicity of language." She refers to the existence of neurotic symptoms such as conversion in hysteria as the most potent proof for this fact. According to her, the symptom of conversion implies a regression to a primitive preverbal language that uses corporeal sensations and processes in order to express emotions, desires, and unconscious convictions. It is evident that this interpretation should be compared in great detail with the Lacanian perspective according to which the unconscious actually is very much of the order of signifiers and language.

83. In this context Isaacs also points out that we are dealing with a child who greatly lagged behind in her language development.

However, phantasy is in essence neither visual nor of the order of the image. Even though, according to Klein, the visual image is much more closely linked to unconscious processes, and in its effects precedes verbal expression from a genetic point of view, this does not allow us to characterize phantasy as being in essence visual (Isaacs 1948). On the contrary, phantasy corresponds to a logic of sensation that is more primary than visual images and language, from genetic as well as a structural point of view. In the first instance, according to Klein, phantasy is nothing other than "the affective interpretations of bodily sensations" (Isaacs 1948, p. 88), which initially are not linked to visual or plastic images (Isaacs 1948).[84]

We have already pointed out that the young child immediately interprets every corporeal sensation and feeling. In the young child, sensation, significance, and perception are an as yet inseparable tangle. This is exactly why the child may experience the feeling of hunger immediately as an attack. One may recall the example of bed-wetting (Isaacs 1948), which Klein connects with the aggressive phantasy of the harmful effects of urine and the dangers associated therewith. This does not mean that the child is able to form a concrete idea of the harmful effects of urine. The unpleasurable sensations it experiences while bed-wetting *are*, on the contrary, the "belief" in urine's harmfulness. The corporeal experience is immediately significant or immediately institutes meaning. Initially phantasy is just this affective interpretation (Rivière 1936).[85]

Phantasy becomes progressively more complex when the first memories of corporeal experiences and of external reality are woven into it.

---

84. This explains Julia Kristeva's (1984) interest in Klein's work. Kristeva uses the Kleinian phantasy in order to think about what she calls the "semiotic."

85. About the earliest phantasies, Isaacs writes, for example, that they are primarily related to the oral zone, and linked to taste, smell, touch (of the lips and the mouth), and kinesthetic perceptions. She adds, "These sensations (and images) are a bodily experience, at first scarcely capable of being related to an external, spatial object." In this context one should recall what we have written about the "proto-object"; "they gives the phantasy a concrete bodily quality, a "me-ness," experienced *in* the body. . . . The skin is not yet felt to be a boundary between outer and inner reality" (Isaacs 1948, p. 92).

The dominence of the affect that characterized the phantasy of early child-hood is broken fairly quickly—and in particular with the advent of the depressive position[86]—such that plastic and visual images can also play a role in phantasmatic activity. These images are further linked more and more with the organized perceptions of external reality.

However, this does not mean that phantasies originate in the knowledge of external reality. On the contrary, they come to exist in the body itself, and in particular emerging from the instinct at work in the body. According to Klein (1952), early eating disorders are often related to anxieties linked to the oral instinct. The child is afraid of destroying his or her love object by biting it to pieces. However, one may not deduce from this that such phantasies can only occur once the young child is consciously aware of the fact that biting someone to pieces also means killing or destroying someone. Such a conception misses the core of the problem. It fails to recognize, according to Klein, that this knowledge is inherent in the bodily activities that the instinct uses to realize itself, as well as in the aims of the instinct and the affects that are connected with it (Isaacs 1948). The body knows from out of itself that the oral intake of an object implies its destruction.

We have constantly emphasized the preverbal and even previsual character of the Kleinian phantasy. Phantasy is an affective interpre-tation of a corporeal sensation according to the pleasure principle: what is pleasurable is good, what is unpleasurable is bad and hostile. And yet, in the context of phantasy, Klein often speaks of *imagos*,[87] which permits the suspicion that we are dealing with visual images after all, which give a direction to psychic life.[88] Isaacs (1948), how-ever, writes that the original imago contains all somatic, tactile, and

---

86. We have already pointed out that the advent of the depressive position is indissolubly linked with the development of the perceptive—and in particular the visual—abilities and new cognitive capacities.

87. Laplanche and Pontalis (1967) define imago as follows: "Unconscious pro-totypical figure which orients the subject's way of apprehending others; it is built up on the basis of the first real and phantasied relationships within the family envi-ronment" (p. 211).

88. Klein (1952) often speaks of pictures with regard to the good and bad breast. But we believe that it would be wrong to understand Klein in the same concrete man-

emotional elements from which the relation to the imagined person (or a part thereof) receives its form. These elements provide the phantasy (the imago) with a concrete corporeal quality that is experienced in the body itself. Visual elements then play no role or only a small role in the original imago. The visual element of perception only develops later and goes together with a repression of the original corporeal aspects of phantasy. The somatic and emotional aspects of experience are indeed to a significant extent absent from the image. The relation to the image is to a high degree "dis-incarnated." It is something that we see or place before us, but do not immediately experience within us.[89] We no longer experience in our body what stands before us.[90]

SEXUALITY IN THE WORK OF KLEIN[91]

What is the place of sexuality in Klein's work? The question of the significance of sexuality for human existence plays a much smaller role in Klein's work than it does in the work of Freud. On the contrary, everything revolves around the defense against and the working through of anxiety and aggressivity. We have already pointed out that the relation

---

ner in which she writes. At various points she herself cautions against such objectivizing and concretizing readings.

89. It is clear that any description of these early phantasies cannot but do them injustice since language institutes a distance to the reality that it describes. This distance is not yet present in phantasy.

90. In his texts on the mirror stage (Lacan 1966) as well as in the texts in which he interprets Klein (for example, Lacan 1975), Lacan understands the imago in the Kleinian sense from the perspective of the dynamics of the mirror image. In light of our exposé, this equation appears as highly problematic.

91. In what follows we do not provide an exhaustive treatment of the Oedipus complex and sexuality in the work of Klein. We limit ourselves to what is strictly necessary for our problematic. For example, we will not take into consideration Klein's (interesting) reflections on the different courses taken by the Oedipus complex in girls and boys. We shall also not consider the evolution of Klein's thought on this subject, but rather limit ourselves to her later thought on this issue. For further commentary on sexuality and the Oedipus complex in the work of Klein, see Klein 1928, 1945, 1952, Heimann 1955, and Green 1990.

between erogenous experiences of pleasure and sexuality hardly worries Klein as an important theoretical problem. When speaking about sexuality, Klein in the first place thinks about the development of the genital libido in the Oedipus complex (Klein 1932). In contrast to Freud, she situates the first development of genital organization (and the Oedipus complex that is linked with it) in very early childhood, and in fact already even in the paranoid-schizoid position. In so doing, a number of elements are important. First, the reference to the penis of the father—which, according to Klein, is supposed to be present very early on—implies that in the first months of life a minimal "triangulation" must already take place.[92] Second, Klein thinks that in the same period the first impulses for the creation of the superego are also already at work. The good breast (which rewards and supports me) and the bad breast (which persecutes me) are foreshadowings of the positive and negative aspects of the later superego. In this manner, Klein reverses a crucial Freudian perspective. According to Freud, the superego only comes about at the end of the oedipal period as the result of the internalization of the parental figures that takes place in this period (Freud 1923). In Klein, on the other hand, the first impulses to the formation of the superego are already given before the start of the Oedipus complex in the proper sense. The advent of the latter is intrinsically interwoven with the problematic of the depressive position. Klein understands and thematizes it in terms of the general problematic of her metapsychology. What does this mean?

In Kleinian metapsychology the loss of the object plays a central role. It is the absence of the breast that gives a hostile and aggressive color to the world in the paranoid-schizoid position, against which the child must defend him- or herself. And it is the absence of the mother that during the depressive position creates the anxiety that we have damaged her through our aggressivity, or have even destroyed her. Evidently, the Oedipus complex too can be understood in the light of

---

92. Perhaps we can link this to the fact that the young child already experiences from very early on a difference in the way in which the father and the mother deal with it.

the inevitable loss of the object. The child who thinks that it is able to exercise an exclusive claim on the mother must recognize that the mother's desires are not only limited to it. It has to recognize that it must share the mother with the father. In this respect the problematic of the Oedipus complex connects seamlessly with the general thematic of Kleinian psychoanalysis. In contrast to Freud, who considers the significance of the Oedipus complex from the perspective of the development of libido toward genital adult sexuality, Klein understands the Oedipus complex in the first instance from the perspective of the loss of the object for which it provides a reason. After all, the advent of the Oedipus complex means that the absence of the object is from that moment on viewed in the light of a rivalry with another object. This is an important step in dealing with primitive anxiety. The absence of the object is no longer a mere catastrophe that overcomes you, which you do not understand, and of which you have no grasp. The absence of the object, on the contrary, places you in a position of rivalry with an (equally loved) object: the father.

Analogously, Klein sees castration anxiety as a concretization of the fear of death[93]: According to Klein male genitalia are not only the source of an intense libidinous experience of pleasure, but also represent the life instincts. Furthermore, reproduction is a way to resist death. Consequently, Klein concludes that the loss of this body part equals for the infant the loss of the creative force that protects and continues life (Klein 1948). That which at first was a "nameless dread" (Bion) becomes anxiety of castration and a recognizable danger against which you may defend yourself in a more or less adequate fashion.

The Oedipus complex contributes to a transformation of primitive anxieties. At the same time it is intrinsically interwoven with the paranoid-schizoid and depressive positions. For the Oedipus complex presupposes that the young child is able to relate to total objects and able to recognize their (relative) independence. The Oedipus complex further implies a recognition of the ambivalent feelings toward one and

---

93. "The anxiety of death enters into and reinforces castration anxiety" (Klein 1948, p. 30).

the same object: father and mother are loved as well as hated.[94] In this way the development of the oedipal problematic is made codependent on the dynamics of both subjective positions. The Oedipus complex not only offers an answer to primitive anxiety: its content and its course are likewise determined by these anxieties and the manner in which we may deal with them (Klein 1945).[95]

According to Klein, the Oedipus complex originates in a strengthening of genital desires toward the parents at around the middle of the first year of life. These genital impulses are initially still strongly linked with oral, anal, and urethral instincts and phantasies of a libidinous and aggressive nature. The destructive energy emerging from these sources is still further reinforced by the psychotic anxieties connected thereto, which may complicate oedipal development significantly. Hence, the libidinous development is at every moment influenced by the anxiety's characteristic for the paranoid-schizoid and depressive positions. The desire to penetrate the mother may be experienced as an aggressive attack on the inside of her body and give rise to the anxiety of being persecuted by the mother but also by the "bad" penis of the father, the presence of which the small child suspects in the mother. For example, Klein (1945) also relates the story of Richard, who could not bear his ambivalence toward his mother. He solves this problem by making a strict distinction between a good breast mother and a bad genital mother, upon which his sexual desires were directed, and who had abandoned him. Richard fears the revenge of the bad genital mother, who in the analysis is represented by Klein. In this fashion Richard

---

94. Laplanche and Pontalis (1967) define the Oedipus complex as follows: "Organized body of loving and hostile wishes which the child experiences toward its parents. In its so-called *positive* form, the complex appears as in the story of *Oedipus Rex*, a desire for the death of the rival—the parent of the same sex—and a sexual desire for the parent of the opposite sex. In its *negative* form, we find the reverse picture: love for the parent of the same sex and jealous hatred for the parent of the opposite sex. In fact the two versions are to be found in varying degrees in the *complete* form of the complex" (p. 282).

95. "Both persecutory and depressive anxiety contribute fundamentally to the conflicts arising in the oedipal situation and influence a libidinal development" (Klein 1952, p. 81).

regressed into a paranoid-schizoid manner of functioning. These two simple examples already show sufficiently that the oedipal problematic is experienced in function of the subjective positions that Klein distinguishes.

In this context we may also recall Klein's study of little Dick, which we discussed earlier in this chapter. Klein links Dick's mutism with the premature advent of the genital phase. As a result the genital impulses are entirely experienced in function of the problematic of the paranoid-schizoid position and in particular of the sadism that reigns supreme in it. In Dick's estimate, his penis was the most important organ of his sadism, against which he had to defend himself. The repression of genitality and of the oedipal impulses resulted. His anxiety was so great that the oedipal development simply could not take place.

But we must not conclude that libidinous development is only negatively influenced by paranoid-schizoid and depressive anxieties. From the case study of little Dick we know that anxiety also has a positive significance for the development of the subject. Indeed, the necessity of dealing with anxiety and of defending against it is an important impetus for psychic as well as libidinous development. Here all is a question of degree. On the one hand, anxiety is a necessary factor in the development of the ego. On the other hand, anxiety must not be too great—or the ego's tolerance for anxiety too low—so that the development of the small child will not be impaired. The development of libido is therefore constantly influenced by anxiety in a positive as well as a negative sense (Klein 1952).

We have to make this last point more specific. Anxiety—but also guilt and the tendency to reparation, which are crucial elements of the depressive position—according to Klein plays a role in libidinous development. The need to transform anxiety and to find an adequate answer to it compels the child to develop further. Oedipal conflicts are like a laboratory in which the child can learn to deal with anxiety and feelings of guilt. The giving and receiving of libidinous gratification lessens anxiety and satisfies the tendency toward reparation. The complex oedipal relations toward the father and the mother teach the child that hate and love are not absolute opposites and that her "preference" for the father does not mean that her love for the child has disappeared.

After some time the child also realizes, for example, that his aggressivity toward the father does not mean that the latter now rejects and hates him for all time. Klein (1952) concludes, "In the process of the Oedipus conflicts and achieving genital primacy the child becomes able to establish its good object securely in his inner world and to develop a stable relation to his parents. All this means that he is gradually working through and modifying persecutory and depressive anxiety" (p. 83). The oedipal problematic protects us from and contributes to the solution for primitive anxieties that threaten the child.[96]

CONCLUSION

Like Freud in his later texts, Klein replaces the original psychoanalytic theory of the primacy of sexuality with a theory of the primacy of the child and of the trauma. This trauma no longer has a sexual nature. Klein, on the contrary, understands it as the effect of the inner workings of the death instinct. The further psychic development and in particular psychosexual development is a way of dealing with the anxiety and aggressivity that are an answer to this first trauma. We have interpreted the Kleinian death instinct just as we have previously interpreted the Freudian death instinct as a superfluous concept that in principle refers to the helplessness of children with regard to their own aggressivity and with regard to the satisfaction of their vital needs. Like Freud, Klein reduces this dimension to its most elementary components: hunger and thirst. This means that she understands all other links between the child and the surrounding reality—in the first instance with the mother—as secondary to and derived from these basic needs. The child loves the mother because he is fed by her. "Love" is in a metonymical relation to "milk." Furthermore, we have seen how the object

---

96. In a certain sense the latter is also the case in the work of Lacan. Lacan too sees sexuality and the Oedipus complex—which, in contrast to Klein, he links to the symbolic order of signifiers—as a defense against incipient psychotic anxieties. In terms of inspiration, the work of the later Freud, of Klein, and of Lacan are much closer to one another than is often suspected. For the status of sexuality and the Oedipus complex in the work of Lacan, see Van Haute 2004.

relations as such are, according to Klein, already a first answer to the anxiety that arises from the traumatic activities of the death instinct.[97] In her case study of little Dick, Klein demonstrates how a meaningful reality can be constituted in a metonymic manner out of the inner necessity of dealing with anxiety. The reformulation of the theory of the death instinct in terms of the infantile helplessness toward its own instincts and of a vital trauma in essence changes nothing about this. In this reformulated theory of the death instinct too, object relations and attachment are conceived as an answer to a trauma and to negative vital experiences.

This confronts us with two problems. First, it is very problematic to make the relation to reality and in particular to the other dependent on a trauma from which it can be deduced. Is the relation to the other then not original? Must it be based on a more primitive fact? Second, it is not self-evident that we should exclusively understand the vital relation to the other and the instinct of self-preservation in terms of hunger and thirst, such as Klein and Freud do. Does the young child not have needs other than merely eating and drinking? Furthermore, these problems are closely related. Hunger and thirst, after all, are negative experiences. When one seeks to understand the vital relation to the other exclusively on the basis of these negative experiences, it is almost inevitable to understand this relation as an answer to them and as their effect: the infant seeks the proximity of the mother because it is hungry and thirsty. Freud and Klein, then, are only consequent when they reduce the attachment of the child to the mother and our later need to be loved to the basic experience of helplessness and dependency that is said to be its biological source.[98]

---

97. This implies that Kleinian psychoanalysis may not simply be understood as an object-relation theory. After all, according to Klein, the instinct does not look for an object out of itself but in answer to and as a defense against primitive situations of anxiety (Klein 1948).

98. Freud (1926), for example, writes, "The reason why the infant at arms wants to perceive the presence of its mother is only because it already knows by experience that she satisfies all its needs without delay. The situation then, which it regards as a "danger" and against which it wants to be safeguarded is that of non-satisfaction, of a growing tension due to need, against which it is helpless" (p. 137).

Attachment, as well as the need to be loved, are secondary instincts for Freud and Klein.[99]

This approach has been vehemently protested by John Bowlby, who describes a series of behaviors of the young child, such as seizing, smiling, shouting, weeping, and looking, but also separation anxiety, curiosity, anger, and sadness, as attachment behavior. This means that these behaviors aim at the proximity of the mother. According to Bowlby, this interest in the proximity of the mother is original and irreducible. It is inherent in the biological nature of humanity. The attachment to and interest in an external object—in the first instance, the mother[100]—cannot fully be explained on the basis of the sexual instinct and the concern for self-preservation. Bowlby consequently rejects the Freudian and Kleinian perspective, according to which the proximity of the mother is merely the guarantee for a full stomach. Attachment behavior cannot be reduced to a too narrowly defined instinct of self-preservation.

What does this mean for our reformulation of the Freudian and Kleinian theory of the death instinct? In our reformulation too, attachment behavior is explained as an answer to a vital trauma and therefore as a secondary instinct. This standpoint, however, is difficult to defend. The sphere of attachment has a *sui generis* character and as such we must attempt to assign it a place in psychoanalysis. We therefore are compelled to take yet another step in our reasoning and to amend the Freudian and Kleinian model further. We must ask ourselves the question of how we may integrate the problematic of attachment in psychoanalytic metapsychology without denigrating the primacy of the

---

99. This does not mean that in Klein's work any reference to attachment as a primary domain of human existence is lacking. We shall return to this point in Chapter 3.

100. We must remark at this point that infantile attachment behavior is in the first instance not aimed at an object. The theory of attachment is not an object-relation theory. What the child looks for is in the first instance a physical state, the maintenance of the desired degree of proximity to the mother. This physical goal is later replaced by a more psychological goal, feeling of bonding or closeness. Therefore, attachment behavior is not primarily directed at an object but at a state of being or a feeling (Fonagy 2001).

child and trauma and without having to abandon the project of a clinical anthropology.

For this emendation we will consult the Hungarian psychoanalyst Imre Hermann. In an important article from 1936 on *Sich Anklammern—Auf Suche gehen* ["Clinging—Searching"], Hermann develops a theory of attachment, which, he claims, offers an answer to the clinical problems that forced Freud to formulate the hypotheses of the death instinct such as the status of aggressivity, masochism, and the compulsion to repeat. Therefore, this article is eminently suitable to elaborate in detail the problems that our own interpretation of Freud and Klein confront us with. First we will subject the critique of the work of Freud and Klein by the theorists of attachment—and in particular Bowlby—to closer investigation. This is not only meant to enable us further to specify the problematic to which Chapter 3 seeks an answer, but it will also make clear why the psychoanalytic tradition has always been wary of the theory of attachment.

3

Between Detachment
and Inconsolability:
Toward a Clinical
Anthropology
of Attachment

We have analyzed the death instinct as the compulsive repetition of infantile traumas during the later course of life. We have shown how the traumatic core of the unconscious, which is based on the radical helplessness of the baby, is modified by anal erotization and the castration complex and is as such repeated in our relation to others, fate, and death. We have also discussed how the primitive reactions of the child to this traumatic helplessness are described by Melanie Klein in terms of psychoses. In the depressive and the paranoid-schizoid position the early ego assumes a position toward the instinctual dangers that threaten to overwhelm it. We have emphasized that the helplessness of infants is in the final analysis a radical helplessness in the face of their own instincts. In Freud as well as Klein these are in the first instance the instincts of self-preservation, such as hunger and thirst. Klein also adds that children are equally powerless against their own aggression (see The Repetition of Primitive Catastrophes in Chapter 1; see also Chapter 2). These instincts not only threaten pleasure, but existence as such. According to Freud and Klein, these very basic experiences of helplessness, dependence, and aggression constitute the biological source of the attachment of the child to the mother and of our later need to be loved.

It would be a mistake to think that we have already sufficiently defined Freud's and Klein's insights on the metapsychological status of attachment. Not only do they make attachment or partial aspects of attachment their explicit theme of reflection in various places in their works, but also their insights on the subject show an important evolution over time. We will first discuss the Freudian and the Kleinian theories of attachment and their respective historical evolution. We confront the Freudian and the Kleinian metapsychology of attachment at the same time with Bowlby's critique thereof, in order to clarify why Freud and

Klein did not succeed unambiguously in integrating attachment within their theories of the instinct. Thus it also becomes possible to determine the crucial points of difference between psychoanalysis and attachment theory.

In doing so it is not our aim to simply raise one theory above the other. Bowlby's justified rejection of the Freudian and Kleinian approach to the problematic of attachment does not prevent him from presupposing a naive concept of time, as well as a traditional distinction between normality and pathology, ensuring that his critique bore no further fruit for psychoanalysis. To remove this objection we will consult the Hungarian psychoanalyst Imre Hermann, who develops a Freudian theory of attachment that at the same time provides an answer to the clinical impasses of the Freudian and the Kleinian death instinct. A reading of Hermann's (1936) essay *Sich Anklammern—Auf Suche gehen* will enable us to reconcile the problematic of attachment with the model of trauma that we have defended until now. We shall demonstrate that the Freudian–Kleinian problematic of the death instinct can only adequately be addressed from the perspective of a clinical anthropology of attachment.

ATTACHMENT IN THE WORK OF FREUD

Bowlby criticizes Freud from a theoretical as well as from a methodological perspective. On a theoretical level Bowlby accuses Freud of being able only to see the attachment of the child to the adult as a secondary instinct. Freudian psychoanalysis does not perceive attachment as an original dimension of human existence. For the child the attachment to the mother is ultimately just a guarantee that its vital needs will be satisfied.[1] Freud (1926) also conceives of separation anxiety as

---

1. Bowlby describes Freud's concept of attachment as follows: "The child has a number of physiological needs which must be met, particularly for food and warmth. In so far as the baby becomes interested in and attached to a human figure, especially the mother, this is the result of the mother's meeting the baby's physiological needs and the baby's learning in due course that she is the source of his gratifications. I shall call this the theory of Secondary Drive" (Bowlby 1969, p. 178).

a signal of the repetition of the primitive catastrophe of the tension caused by various needs (see A Death Instinct? in Chapter 1). From a methodological perspective Bowlby (1973) is of the opinion that childhood would be better known and studied by direct observation, rather than by reconstruction through the analysis of adults as Freud thought (Fonagy 2001).

We will first discuss the problematic of attachment in Freud and Klein, and demonstrate that Freud's analysis of aggression and curiosity is dominated by the same theoretical problems as his discussion of the problematic of attachment. Subsequently we will deal with Bowlby's methodological complaints against Freudian and Kleinian psychoanalysis.

Attachment and Loss

According to Bowlby the attachment of the child to the mother must not be understood in terms of helplessness and dependency. The sphere of attachment is original. To be attached to someone or something is something other than to be dependent thereupon. This is clearly evident in the observation of children. In truth, during the first months of life the newborn is indeed radically dependent on the mother for his self-preservation, but during this period there cannot yet be talk of any attachment to the mother or attachment behavior. In its behavior the child does not yet make a distinction between acquaintances and strangers. According to Bowlby it is only later, at around six months, that the child demonstrates all kinds of behaviors that indicate that he is interested in the proximity of the mother and that he reacts to the absence of the mother with separation anxiety (Bowlby 1969).[2] Freud's assumption that children's interest in the presence of the mother is only based on their biological dependency on her lacks any empirical proof (Bowlby 1969). On the contrary, we may find similar attachment behavior in

---

2. We are not concerned with affirming or denying Bowlby's findings with recent research. We merely wish to point out that Bowlby points to a domain of existence that has been neglected by Freud.

higher primates, even if they do not have as long a period of dependency on the mother as humans do (Bowlby 1969). Would it not be strange if a whole series of behaviors and feelings that occur in most mammals— and in higher primates in a manner very similar to that of humans—would in the latter have to be explained in an entirely other fashion than in animals? Furthermore, children may also be attached to persons who are not at all occupied with the satisfaction of their needs.

Today the general tenor of Bowlby's critique appears almost self-evident to us; rather, it is surprising that Freud could have remained so blind to this dimension of human nature. This blindness to the originality of the problematic of attachment is the result of Freud's dualism of the instinct. In view of the fact that for Freud there are only two primary instincts, the instinct of self-preservation and the sexual instinct, all behaviors and tendencies that, according to Bowlby, belong to the domain of attachment and loss can be reduced to either one of these two instincts or to a combination of the two (Freud 1915a). An analysis of the historical development of Freud's insights on attachment does indeed show that he never succeeded in unambiguously situating this problematic in his dualistic theory of the instinct. This inability to do so is a symptom of the limitations of his dualistic theory of the instinct. What is at stake is to assign to the problematic of attachment the original place proper to it.

In his *Three Essays on the Theory of Sexuality*, Freud (1905b) asserts that the attachment of the child to the mother has a sexual origin. Initially the sexual instincts are attached to the vital functions of the child. Oral erotism is attached to the satisfaction of hunger, anal erotism to the function of excretion. But in thumb-sucking and anal masturbation, infantile sexuality becomes autoerotic. The search for pleasure, after all, does not stop with the satisfaction of a need. Once hunger is satisfied, the baby starts to suck its thumb in order to continue the pleasure that has been evoked in sucking the breast (Freud 1905b).[3] That the sexual instinct becomes autoerotic does not mean that children no longer have any interest in the persons in their surrounding: throughout the period of latency children learn to feel

---

3. See Van Haute and Geyskens 2004.

for people who help them in their helplessness and satisfy their needs of love, which is both modeled on, as well as a continuation of, their relation as sucklings to their nursing mother (Freud 1905a). Therefore, in 1905 Freud assumes that the tender relations of the child with persons in its environment are based on tempered sexual interests.[4] In the *Three Essays*, separation anxiety too is viewed as a sexual anxiety: "In this respect a child, by turning his libido into anxiety when he cannot satisfy it, behaves just like an adult" (Freud 1905b, p. 224).

In *Mourning and Melancholia*, Freud (1917b), however, encounters another difficulty, which appears to cast doubt on his conception of the sexual origin of attachment. According to Freud, the work of mourning consists of relinquishing a libidinous attachment because the object of this attachment has died or has been lost as a love object. The work of mourning goes together with a "painful unpleasure" (*Schmerzunlust*) (Freud 1917b, p. 245). In *Mourning and Melancholy* Freud is unable to explain why mourning is so painful. This inability is the consequence of his sexual theory of attachment. Freud always emphasizes that the object of the sexual instinct is extremely variable and interchangeable. In *Instincts and their Vicissitudes*, Freud (1915a) writes, "It [the object] is what is most variable about an instinct and is not originally connected with it, but becomes assigned to it only in consequence of being peculiarly fitted to make satisfaction possible" (p. 122). On the basis of the pleasure principle there is no reason why we should not replace one satisfying object with another without any difficulty. In his study of mourning and melancholy, however, Freud is confronted with the fact that we can only let go of a lost libidinous object and replace it with a new object, by means of the work of mourning and a "painful feeling of unpleasure."[5] This too is self-evident, even for Freud, but his libido theory cannot explain the painful character of mourning.

---

4. "Children themselves behave from an early age as though their dependence [*Anhänglichkeit*] on the people looking after them were in the nature of sexual love" (Freud 1905b, p. 224).

5. "All around us one may perceive that man does not like to abandon a libidinal position even if a substitute is already waiting for him" (Freud 1917b, pp. 306–307)..

The theoretical embarrassment is expressed in Freud's use of the curious term *Schmerzunlust*. This tautological expression is a symptom of Freud's problem of distinguishing pain (*Schmerz*) from unpleasure (*Unlust*). We have already discussed Freud's idea that neurotic unpleasure must be understood as "pleasure which cannot be experienced as such" (see Chapter 1). But, as with posttraumatic anxiety, the pain of mourning may also not be considered as repressed pleasure. Mourning is quite a different kind of affect than for example shame, which is based on the repression of an exhibitionist tendency (Freud 1905b). Freud (1920) only addresses this specific difference between pain and unpleasure in *Beyond the Pleasure Principle*. He distinguishes painful experiences that could never have been pleasurable from neurotic unpleasure, in which "what could have been a possibility for pleasure is perceived by the ego as unpleasure" (p. 11). Freud's reflections on pain in *Beyond the Pleasure Principle* lead him to develop a new theory of attachment in *Inhibitions, Symptoms, and Anxiety* (Freud 1926), in which the attachment of the child to the mother is no longer based on infantile sexuality but on the biological helplessness of the baby. In *Inhibitions, Symptoms, and Anxiety*, Freud no longer considers the anxiety of separation to be transformed libido, but a signal of the anticipation of a traumatic situation of a tension of needs (see Chapter 1). The child experiences the absence of the mother as the buildup for the situation of hunger and helplessness. Attachment is in the first instance anxiously being on guard against the repetition of this primitive catastrophe (Freud 1926).

Freud reduces attachment either to the sexual instinct or to the experiences linked to self-preservation and helplessness. In both cases attachment is a secondary instinct or the modification of a more original primal instinct. Freud has even greater difficulty unambiguously to determine the status of the instinct of mastery and that of curiosity as it occurs in the complex interplay of the sexual instinct and the instinct of self-preservation.[6] After all, in his analyses of the instinct of mastery and of curiosity Freud again encounters the problem of attachment to

---

6. We have already pointed out that according to Bowlby mastery and curiosity must be counted in the domain of attachment. Hermann thinks no differently. (We shall return to this point.)

an object that can hardly be understood adequately on the basis of his dualism of the instinct. We will discuss these difficulties in light of the historical evolution of Freud's reflections on the instinct of mastery and curiosity.

The Instinct of Mastery and Curiosity

In *Three Essays on the Theory of Sexuality*, Freud (1905b) explicitly claims that the instinct of mastery is originally not sexual, even if this instinct is extraordinarily well suited for the service of sexuality. Sexual aggression is not simply a component of the sexual instinct, but it is based on the sexualization of the "apparatus for obtaining mastery, which is concerned with the satisfaction of the other and, ontogenetically, the older of the great instinctual needs" (Freud 1905b, p. 159). The instinct of mastery is originally in the service of self-preservation and only becomes sexual in a second step. In a passage that is only included in the first edition of the *Three Essays*, Freud refers to the ambiguous status of mastery as follows:

> It may be assumed that the impulses of cruelty arise from sources which are *in fact independent* of sexuality, but may become united with it at an early stage owing to an anastomosis [cross-connection] near their points of origin. Observation teaches us, however, that sexual development and the development of the instinct of scopophilia and cruelty are subject to mutual influences which limit this *presumed independence* of the two sets of instincts. [Freud 1905b, p. 193, italics added]

Consequently in the first edition of the *Three Essays* Freud situated the instinct of mastery and aggression between sexuality and self-preservation. The same is true for the instinct to know, or curiosity.

In the *Three Essays* Freud calls curiosity a sublimated form of mastery. Curiosity, too, "cannot be counted among the elementary instinctual components, nor can it be classed as exclusively belonging to sexuality" (Freud 1905b, p. 194). Like attachment, curiosity too is a secondary instinct. Freud suggests that the origin of curiosity is rooted in the problematic of attachment: "*The threat to the bases of a child's existence* offered by the discovery or the suspicion of the arrival of a new baby and the fear that he may, as a result of it, *cease to be cared for and loved*, make him thoughtful and clear-sighted" (Freud 1905b, pp. 194–195, italics added). The pregnancy of the mother and the birth of a new baby stimulate the child's curiosity. However, we are not dealing with an innate need that belongs to the child's nature and requires no further explanation. On the contrary, curiosity arises because it is based on the anxiety of children to lose—at least partially—the care of the mother, and that the object to which they are attached might abandon them.[7] These fears themselves are based on "the threat to the bases of a child's existence." After all, the existence of the child depends on the care and love of the mother. Curiosity, then, is in principle "the product of a vital exigency" (Freud 1908b, p. 213). It is first directed toward things that endanger the existence of the child. Because the arrival of a new baby threatens the bond between the child and the mother, the child directs his curiosity to the riddles of adult sexuality. In this way the instinct to know is quickly linked to sexuality. In the *Three Essays*, Freud consequently assumes that even though the instinct of mastery and curiosity are well suited to become sexualized, they do not have a sexual origin. Originally they are at the service of self-preservation.

In *Instincts and Their Vicissitudes*, Freud (1915a) discusses the instinct of mastery and curiosity anew, but at first sight the previous ambiguity has disappeared. In his analysis of sadomasochism, Freud asserts that "sadism consists in the exercise of violence or power upon some other person as object" (p. 127). This definition of sadism no longer contains a reference to its sexual character. The subtle difference between the mastery of the object in the service of self-preservation and the sexual aggression of sadism that Freud had still emphasized in *Three Essays* has

---

7. "A child's desire for knowledge on this point does not in fact awaken spontaneously, prompted perhaps by some inborn need for established causes; it is aroused under the goad of the self-seeking instincts that dominate him when—perhaps at the end of his second year—he is confronted with the arrival of a new baby" (Freud 1908b, p. 212).

now disappeared in *Instincts and Their Vicissitudes*. Freud now considers every form of aggression to be (sexual) sadism. In contrast to his earlier conception that sadism only arises by a sexualization of the instinct of mastery, Freud in *Instincts and Their Vicissitudes* assigns the instinct of mastery as such to sexuality. The same is true for curiosity or the instinct to look. While in the *Three Essays* and *On the Sexual Theories of Children* (Freud 1908b), Freud had emphasized that the instinct to look and know arose from a "practical" need and "self-serving" motives (Freud 1908b, p. 212), in *Instincts and Their Vicissitudes*, Freud identifies the instinct to look with voyeurism. Freud defines voyeurism as "looking as an activity directed towards an extraneous object" (Freud 1915a, p. 129). There too he no longer distinguishes between the sexual pleasure of looking and curiosity. In *Instincts and Their Vicissitudes*, the entire dimension of attachment, aggression, and curiosity is absorbed by sexuality. The references to need, the maintenance of one's own existence and helplessness, disappear from Freud's theory, at least for the time being. However, this confronts Freud with an important theoretical problem. When he calls the instinct sexual, this means that at the least this instinct can also be satisfied autoerotically and without an object. The lips and the anus are the prototypical erogenous zones from which the instinct arises. Via food and excretion, pleasure is caused in these zones, which in a second instance can be sought for the sake of itself. In this way, autoerotic sexuality arises, which has no need of an object.[8] In sucking, the lips, as it were, discover that they can attain pleasure from themselves without an object: "'It's a pity I can't kiss myself,' he seems to be saying" (Freud 1905b, p. 182). In *Instincts and Their Vicissitudes*, Freud radicalizes this insight by describing a narcissistic primal state in which instincts that out of themselves refer to an object are originally also satisfied by one's own body.

The identification of the instinct of mastery with sadism and the instinct to look with voyeurism forces Freud to include hands and eyes in the series of erogenous zones, along with the mouth, the anus,

---

8. On this point see Sexuality in the Work of Klein in Chapter 2 and *Confusion of Tongues*, Van Haute and Geyskens 2004.

and the genital zone. They are, after all, the erogenous sources of sadism and voyeurism. It is, however, utterly unclear how the pleasure that eye and hand can obtain for us can be conceived of in terms of an autoerotic and objectless self-affection. However, the possibility of an autoerotic self-affection belongs in essence to the Freudian sexual instinct. In this context, Freud writes,

> In general we can assert of them that their activities are *auto-erotic*; that is to say their object is negligible in comparison with the organ which is their source and as a rule coincides with that organ. The object of the scopophilic instinct, however, though it too is in the first instance a part of the subject's own body, is not the eye itself, and in sadism the organic source which is probably the muscular apparatus with its capacity for action, points unequivocally at an object other than itself, even though that object is part of the subject's own body. [1915a, p. 132, italics Freud]

Freud's equation of the instinct of mastery and curiosity with sadism and voyeurism also forces him to face the possibility of an autoerotic satisfaction of these instincts. He at the same time realizes that sadism and voyeurism cannot be described without some reference to a foreign object, even though Freud writes that this object belongs "to one's own body." But this appears to be a desperate attempt to safeguard his idea of autoerotism as pure self-affection. His remarks, after all, do not take away from the fact that the instinct to look is of itself related to an object and never functions in a merely autoerotic fashion. The relation between the instinct of mastery and curiosity on the one hand and sexuality on the other hand consequently remains ambiguous. In contrast to the lips and the anus, hands and eyes refer out of themselves to an object. In *Instincts and Their Vicissitudes*, however, Freud does not pursue this further and assumes that curiosity may be identified with voyeurism and the instinct of mastery with sadism.

The incorporation of the instinct of mastery and curiosity in sexuality confronts Freud with yet another problem. Sexuality threatens to become the only primal instinct from which all other instincts arise. In order not to lapse into a pan-sexual monism, in *Beyond the Pleasure Principle*, Freud (1920) hence introduces a new dualism of the instinct:

psychic life is dominated by an opposition of eros and thanatos. In *Beyond the Pleasure Principle*, Freud regards all phenomena of the instinct as a mixture of erotism and death instinct. In this way he restores his original intuition that not all psychic activities have a sexual origin, even though they cannot be understood apart from sexuality. Why, however, is Freud so concerned about not falling into a monism of the instinct? Why is a dualistic theory of the instinct so important to psychoanalysis?

A pan-sexualism entails that instincts that are essentially directed toward a foreign object such as attachment, mastery, and curiosity are sexual instincts. This would mean that their objects are of minor importance. In principle, any object can satisfy the sexual instinct. In his theory of sexuality, Freud does indeed stress continually that "the nature and importance of the sexual object recedes into the background" (Freud 1905b, p. 149). The latter implies immediately for Freud that these instincts can be fulfilled by one's own body where they are originally satisfied (Freud 1915a). The notion of a narcissistic primal state, to which we have already referred, carries this train of thought to its ultimate conclusion. In this context Freud writes, "Originally at the very beginning of mental life, the ego is cathected with instincts and is to some extent capable of satisfying them on itself. We call this condition 'narcissism' and this way of obtaining satisfaction 'auto-erotic'" (Freud 1915a, p. 134). Thereby Freud constructs a primal situation that is difficult to imagine in which not only oral and anal instincts but also attachment,[9] aggression, and curiosity are originally satisfied on one's own body.[10]

The introduction of the death instinct in *Beyond the Pleasure Principle* (Freud 1920) corrects the pan-sexual tendency found in *Instincts*

---

9. "If for the moment we define loving as the relation of the ego to its sources of pleasure, the situation *in which the ego loves itself only and is indifferent to the external world* illustrates the first of the opposites which we found to 'loving'" (Freud 1915a, p. 135, italics added).

10. This also explains why Freud in *Instincts and Their Vicissitudes* can only count very basic needs such as hunger and thirst among the instincts of self-preservation and why he must later reduce helplessness to these basic needs.

and Their Vicissitudes (Freud 1915a). In *Beyond the Pleasure Principle,* Freud (1920) designs a philosophy of nature that is dominated by the struggle between Eros and the death instinct. Whereas Freud in this way restores the dualism of instincts, the death instinct remains very abstract and general. We also know (see The First Taboo, in Chapter 1) that thanks to this new theory of the instinct, Freud succeeds in reaffirming the non-sexual character of aggression (instinct of mastery) in *The Economic Problem of Masochism* (Freud 1924) and that in *Inhibition, Symptoms, and Anxiety* (Freud 1926), he is able to link the attachment to the mother back to a biological helplessness of the baby and no longer to sexuality.[11] In *The Economic Problem of Masochism,* Freud writes that aggression arises out of the deflection of the death instinct onto objects in the external world. Only in a second instance can this aggression be put at the service of the sexual instinct as sadism (Freud 1924). In this way Freud returns via the introduction of the death instinct to his original idea that sadism presupposes a sexualization of an—in and of itself not sexual—instinct of mastery.

Discussion

The analysis of the evolution of Freud's thought on attachment, aggression, and curiosity makes it evident that Freud only sees these instincts as secondary instincts that, depending on the period in Freud's work, can be reduced to sexual pleasure or to anxiety about one's self-preservation. This is why Freud never succeeds in giving a convincing analysis of this phenomenon. Bowlby's critique consequently refers to a problem that has been insufficiently thematized by Freud because it cannot be integrated in his dualistic theory of the instinct. Attachment, aggression (instinct of mastery), and curiosity refer to an aspect of instinctual human life that cannot be considered merely sexual but that also cannot be reduced to the most basic interests of hunger, thirst, and prac-

---

11. See Chapter 1. After 1920, Freud no longer speaks of the scopophilic instinct and curiosity.

tical need. Freud's dualism of sexuality and self-preservation causes him difficulty with regard to the problematic of attachment, which "cannot be counted among the elementary instinctual components, nor can it be classed as exclusively belonging to sexuality" (Freud 1905b, p. 194). Freud's attempt to resolve this difficulty by metaphysical speculation on Eros and the death instinct remains abstract and speculative (see Chapter 1). To regard sadism and voyeurism as mixed forms of erotism and death instinct does indeed reestablish the nonsexual component in these expressions of the instinct, but does not contribute any insight into these phenomena.

ATTACHMENT IN THE WORK OF KLEIN

At first sight Klein's theory appears to escape from Freud's problems with attachment. Klein, after all, rejects the thought of a narcissistic primal situation in which instincts are exclusively satisfied by one's own body. The ego as well as an archaic object relation with the breast and later the mother are already present from the outset. And yet, we cannot understand this archaic object relation as a form of attachment. The Kleinian object is, in the first instance, a phantasmatic corporeal experience of satisfaction and frustration of vital needs (see Chapter 2). Klein (1957) describes these object relations in terms of milk and love, and suggests that love is in a metonymic relation with milk. According to Klein, the object relations of children originate in the satisfaction of their vital needs and first and foremost in the anxiety about their frustration.[12] The frustrations of the vital needs confront the early ego with its helplessness and with a powerless anger that it cannot contain.[13] The object relations of

---

12. "For the urge even in the earliest stages to get constant evidence of the mother's love is fundamentally rooted in anxiety" (Klein 1952, p. 179); see Chapter 2.

13. Klein regards the helplessness and the anger of the child as two separate and distinct sources of anxiety: "These two main sources of the infant's fear of loss can be described as follows: one is the child's complete dependence on the mother for the satisfaction of his needs and the relief of tension. . . . The other main source of anxiety derives from the infant's apprehension that the loved mother has been destroyed by his sadistic impulses or is in danger of being destroyed" (Klein 1948, p. 39).

the child are an answer to the helplessness and an attempt to deal with the anger and the fear that follow from it. Like Freud, Klein regards the attachment of the child to the mother as a secondary instinct that is based on the vital needs and the anxiety of helplessness.

However, this does not alter the fact that in Klein's later work there are a number of elements that allow us to expand the concept of infantile object relations. Klein (1959), for example, writes in *Our Adult World and Its Roots in Infancy*:

> My hypothesis is that the infant has an innate unconscious awareness of the existence of the mother. We know that young animals at once turn to the mother and find their food from her. The human animal is not different in that respect, and this instinctual knowledge is the basis for the infant's primal relation to the mother. We can also observe that at an age of only a few weeks the baby already looks up to his mother's face, recognizes her footsteps, the touch of her hands, the smell and feel of her breast or of the bottle that she gives him, all of which suggests that some relation, however primitive, to the mother has been established. [p. 248].

In this and other passages (for example, Klein 1935) Klein is on track to treat attachment as an original biologically inherited link to the mother that no longer has to be deduced ontogenetically from the vital needs and the dependency of the baby. The child is naturally directed toward the proximity of the mother, and this interest is not based on an interest in food.[14] Even though Klein in her later texts alludes repeatedly to the sphere of attachment as an original dimension of human existence, in her metapsychological speculations and analytical interpretations she continues to see attachment as something that is derived from the satisfaction of needs (Klein 1952, 1957).[15] In this way it remains unclear if and to what extent the consequent affirmation of

---

14. Bowlby (1969) correctly points out that feeding plays only a marginal role in the sphere of attachment.

15. In this context, Klein (1952) quotes Margaret Ribble: "This attachment, or, to use the psycho-analytic term, cathexis for the mother grows gradually out of the satisfaction it derives from her" (p. 89).

attachment as an irreducible instinct would have compelled Klein to reformulate her original insights about object relations, the death instinct, and anxiety.

CLINICAL ANTHROPOLOGY VS. DEVELOPMENTAL PSYCHOLOGY

Freud and Klein alike trace the child's attachment to the mother back to the biological dependency of the infant. Bowlby's critique that psychoanalysis does not succeed in seeing attachment as an original irreducible dimension of human nature appears justified. We have already pointed out that attachment behavior also occurs in higher primates and other mammals, even if they do not have a long period of dependency on the mother. Consequently dependency cannot be put forth as an explanation of animal attachment. It is equally improbable that a system of behavior and feelings that can be demonstrated in most mammals would require a different explanation in the case of humans. Bowlby views human attachment behavior, as he does animal attachment behavior, as a phylogenetic product of natural selection and not as a product of the ontogenetic helplessness of the baby (Bowlby 1969, Klein 1959). According to Bowlby, attachment behavior—and more generally the problematic of childhood—should not be reconstructed regressively in the analytical situation, as Freud and Klein thought. On the contrary, Bowlby (1973) wishes to study attachment behavior from the perspective of a progressive development. This means that he wishes to investigate the normal development and the pathological complications of attachment by means of scientific observation from the first year of life until adulthood.[16] Consequently, Bowlby (1973) advances a series of naturalistic studies and empirical investigations in order to describe the development of attachment and the reactions to a situation of loss, from the first year until puberty, and then adulthood. Here

---

16. In this we may recognize what we have called Bowlby's methodological complaints against Freudian–Kleinian psychoanalysis.

we shall not address Bowlby's concrete empirical observations but rather two presuppositions that are inextricably linked with his project:

1. Bowlby presupposes a strict distinction between normal development and pathology. According to Bowlby (1973), later pathologies of attachment are based on earlier traumatic experiences or at least on an inadequate treatment of the child by the adult. In view of the fact that in principle not everyone becomes the victim of a traumatic experience or an inadequate treatment, a normal development that in essence escapes pathology is possible and thinkable.

2. Bowlby presupposes that psychoanalysis reconstructs the development of babies into adults, which he himself in his empirical studies traverses progressively in the opposite direction by means of observations of adults and children. He therefore presupposes a linear perspective of time of development (Bowlby 1973, Fonagy 2001).[17]

We will first discuss Bowlby's concept of the relation between normality and pathology. Then we will address the Freudian–Kleinian concept of time and compare it to Bowlby's.

Normality and Pathology in the Work of Bowlby

In his discussion of psychopathology, Bowlby warns against a possible misunderstanding. In the first place he wants to describe the normal development of normal situations of anxiety: from separation anxiety to the anxiety of strangers until the anxiety of loneliness and the real and imaginary anxieties of adulthood. According to Bowlby (1973), these anxieties can be explained by means of evolutionary theory. They are the result of natural selection and do not require an ontogenetic psy-

---

17. According to Fonagy (2001), Bowlby sees the child as ready to actualize the blueprint of his destiny.

chodynamic explanation. One might expect that in this theory of normal development, pathological anxieties would be thought of as developmental disturbances. This would mean that pathological anxieties do not fit the current phase of development of the subject, whereas they were normal in a previous phase of development. An adult with chronic anxiety toward or suspicion of strangers would, for example, have remained fixed in an earlier stage of development in which these anxieties would have been adequate. According to Bowlby, however, pathologies cannot be explained in this manner. On the contrary, he claims that pathologies are caused by an inappropriate or inadequate response by the environment to the attachment behavior of the child. Pathology is not the regression to a state that once was normal but is now inadequate. It is the consequence of the shortcomings of the mother and the environment during childhood. From this the child learns that a secure attachment cannot be expected, and will—even as an adult—react in accordance with its childhood experience. According to Bowlby, pathological anxieties must therefore be regarded as legitimate products of painful experiences. But they have never been—even in a previous phase—normal.

Bowlby's notion of pathogenesis implies, at least conceptually, a strict distinction between normal development and pathology. Further, it shows some noticeable formal similarities to Freud's theory of seduction in the beginning years of psychoanalysis.[18] Freud, too, initially assumed that pathology could be traced back to a traumatic event or to inappropriate behavior of adults during childhood. All pathologies are the result of seduction of the child by an adult and hence of a sexual trauma. Even though Bowlby's theory of trauma is more complex than Freud's theory of seduction,[19] both start from the assumption that pathology is caused by a specific cause in childhood.[20]

---

18. For an elaborate discussion of the theory of seduction, see Van Haute and Geyskens 2004.

19. "The critical difference between the naïve realism of Freud's early theories and Bowlby's epistemology lies in Bowlby's attention to the representation of experience" (Fonagy 2001, p. 48).

20. Bowlby 1973, *passim*. Fonagy writes: "During the late 70's and 80's, attachment research came to be increasingly concerned with child maltreatment, physical and sexual abuse" (Fonagy 2001, p. 15).

Without this specific cause, no pathology can occur. The primal splitting of normality and pathology results.

Freud abandoned his theory of seduction fairly quickly. This does not mean that he denies that sexual traumas in childhood may have an enormous impact on the later course of life, but it does mean that he projects a new theory, which complicates these traumatic or pathogenic factors immensely. In this new theory, there is no longer any room for a strict distinction between normality and pathology. We shall first briefly expostulate the theory that Freud developed after abandoning the theory of seduction. Then we will show why this theory is irreconcilable with Bowlby's concept of pathogenesis and his concept of the strict distinction between pathology and normality. This irreconcilability is most closely linked to the problematic of temporality.

Puberty and Infantile Sexuality:
Normality and Pathology in Freud

In 1905 Freud published *Fragments of an Analysis of a Case of Hysteria* (1905c). In this work Freud describes the analysis of an 18-year-old girl, Dora, who suffers from hysterical coughing fits and loss of voice. From her story, it appears that these symptoms must be linked to the fact that a friend of her father, Mr. K., had during a stroll asked her to enter into an affair with him, and had, on a previous occasion, attempted to kiss her on the mouth. Dora had reacted to this rather vehemently and demanded that her father discontinue all contact with Mr. and Mrs. K. When her father claims not to be able to respond to this request, she reacts with coughing fits and the loss of her voice. Freud points out that these symptoms had already occurred years before, more specifically when she was 8. He concludes with a reference to his earlier theory of seduction:

> If, therefore, trauma theory is not to be abandoned, we must go back to her childhood and look about there for any influences or impressions which might have had an effect analogous to that of a trauma. Moreover, it deserves to be remarked that in the investigation even of cases in which the first symptoms had not already set in during

childhood, I have been driven to trace back the patients' life history to their earliest years. [Freud 1905c, p. 27]

How are we to understand this? Having abandoned his theory of seduction Freud explicitly considers the quest for childhood trauma to be a false lead. In a letter to Fliess from January 3, 1899, he writes: "To the question what has happened in early childhood, the answer is: nothing, but the germ of a sexual impulse existed" (Freud 1985, p. 338). This implies that the memories of Freud's patient of her early childhood must be understood as fantasies. These phantasies are "products of later periods and are projected back from what was then the present into earliest childhood" (p. 338). According to Freud these screen memories[21] and phantasies about the first years of our life arise in puberty. In the case history of the Ratman (Freud 1909), and in a footnote that was added to the *Three Essays* in 1920, Freud says that our sexual phantasies arise in puberty by means of a deferred (*nachträgliche*) sexualization of innocent and banal occurrences in childhood (Freud 1905b, 1909). Yet this deferred sexualization of memories from childhood is not simply gratuitous phantasizing about the past. The point is not that the adolescent thinks of his current phantasies as old memories. According to Freud (1909), "It at once becomes evident that in his phantasies about his infancy the individual as he grows up *endeavours to efface the recollection of his autoerotic activities*; and this he does by exhalting their memory-traces to the level of object-love, just as a real historian will view the past in the light of the present" (p. 206, italics Freud). Autoerotic experiences of pleasure are translated onto the level of intersubjectivity, which they initially did not possess as infantile experiences of pleasure.[22] We may clarify this by considering the case of Dora.

---

21. Laplanche and Pontalis (1967) define screen memories as follows: "A childhood memory characterized both by its unusual sharpness and by the apparent insignificance of its content. The analysis of such memories leads back to indelible childhood experiences and to unconscious phantasies. Like the symptom, the screen memory is a formation produced by a compromise between repressed elements and defense" (pp. 410–411).

22. "Hence the excess of seductions and assaults that occur in these phantasies while reality is limited to auto-erotic activities and their stimulation by tenderness and punishment" (Freud 1909, p. 44).

In puberty, Dora developed a phantasy of fellatio. This phantasy is what had made Mr. K.'s attempt at seduction so disgusting to her. The complaints of her mouth and throat (loss of voice and coughing fits) were a somatic expression of this phantasy.[23] These phantasies do not indicate that as a child Dora was a victim of oral rape as the theory of seduction would imply. The infantile factor to which Freud traces back Dora's phantasy is the fact that as a child she was a fanatical thumb-sucker: "The somatic preconditions for such an autonomous creation of a phantasy which in its action utterly coincides with that of perverts was in her case given by a noteworthy fact. She remembered very well that in her childhood she had been a thumb-sucker" (Freud 1905c, p. 51). Freud continues, "This excessively repulsive and perverted phantasy of sucking at a penis has the most innocent origin. It is a new version of what may be described as a pre-historic impression of sucking at the mother's or nurse's breast—an impression which has usually been revived by contact with children who are being nursed" (p. 52). The phantasy of fellatio and the hysterical symptoms are therefore not based on a trauma from childhood but on the return in puberty of an infantile experience of pleasure. The renunciation of the theory of seduction led to an extreme de-dramatization of childhood. The perverse phantasies and neurotic symptoms of adults merely go back to a germ of sexual excitement—in the case of Dora, to the oral pleasure of thumb-sucking. Only in the confrontation with adult sexuality during puberty are these innocent infantile experiences of pleasure taken up in sexual phantasies, which, through this return to oral and anal pleasure from childhood, inevitably will display perverse characteristics. Infantile sexuality only receives its psychic significance and instinctual force in puberty.[24]

This short discussion of infantile factors in sexual phantasies of puberty permits us to interpret Freud's (1905b) theory of sexuality

---

23. This does not mean that the phantasy caused the symptoms to arise but that the symptoms received psychic significance (Freud 1905c). (Freud is not Groddeck.)

24. "The sexual life of maturing youth is almost entirely restricted to indulging in phantasies, that is, in ideas that are not destined to be carried into effect. *In these phantasies the infantile tendencies invariably emerge once more, but this time with intensified pressure from somatic sources*" (Freud 1905b, PP. 225–227, italics added).

in *Three Essays on the Theory of Sexuality* correctly. From the analysis of the sexual perversions and neurotic phantasies of adults, Freud arrives at the discovery of infantile sexuality as the germs of sexual excitation.[25] This discovery at the same time implies that a strict distinction between normality and pathology is impossible. According to Freud, these infantile experiences of pleasure are universally human. "The conclusion now presents itself to us that there is indeed something innate lying behind the perversions but that it is something innate in *everyone*" (Freud 1905b, p. 171, italics Freud). The infantile experiences of pleasure return in all people in their sexual phantasies and therefore there is no normal sexuality that does not display one or another perverse characteristic. In sexuality the distinction between normality and pathology is always a distinction of degree (Freud 1905b, Van Haute and Geyskens 2004).

Dora is disgusted by sexuality and by Mr. K.'s dishonorable proposition. Why does she not give in to her phantasy of fellatio and in so doing return to the infantile pleasure of thumb-sucking? Why does she react with disgust to her sexual phantasy and not with perverse pleasure? Freud calls this mechanism of "affect-reversal" reaction formation. Concretely, this means that after a few years have passed the child wants to be a "big boy" and a "good girl" and hence wants to stand above its bad habits. Thus, shame and disgust arise as reaction formations against the infantile experiences of the pleasure of thumb-sucking, anal erotism, and masturbation. The infantile sources of pleasure are being abandoned.[26] It is only at the beginning of puberty

---

25. The Oedipus complex, too, during childhood consists of "seeds of sentiment," which are sexualized retroactively: "Other influences, which need not be discussed here, come into play, and lead to a fixation of this rudimentary feeling of love or to a reinforcement of it; so that it turns into something (either while the child is still young or not until it has reached the age of puberty) which must be put on a par with a sexual inclination and which, like the latter, has the forces of the libido at its command" (Freud 1905c, p. 56). In his later texts about infantile sexuality, Freud appears to abstain from such nuances.

26. Freud also calls this affect-reversal organic repression. The coming about of disgust and shame in a certain moment of development are indeed inherent to human nature (Freud 1905b).

that the conflict between infantile sources of pleasure and reaction formations is reactivated.[27] When reaction formations dominate this conflict, neurosis results. Perversion is the result of the victory of infantile impulses over reaction formations. Dora, for example, became hysterical because she could no longer answer to the confrontation of sexuality in puberty with pleasure, but only with disgust (Freud 1905c). This conflict between reaction formations and perverse impulses is a universal human problem. Just as human sexuality can never be without perverse characteristics, it also cannot exist without an essential relation to shame and disgust (Freud 1905b). For Freud, neurosis and perversion are merely exaggerations of tendencies that characterize human sexuality.

This sketch of Freud's theory of sexuality shows that after he abandoned the theory of seduction, Freud conceived of the relation between normality and pathology in a totally different manner than does Bowlby. In Freud's theory, there is no essential difference between normal development and pathology because Freud thinks of perversion and neurosis as two poles of one continuous spectrum. Normal sexuality can then only be understood in aesthetic terms of harmony and balance and of accident and luck. In Bowlby, on the other hand, normal development is a preprogrammed potential of the child that merely waits to run its course (Fonagy 2001).[28] Indeed, pathology can only be conceived of as a more or less subtle, violent infraction from the outside. Bowlby's trauma model of pathology is the result.

---

27. This conflict can already lead to so-called infantile neuroses in childhood. "This neurosis may last a considerable time and cause marked disturbances, but it may also run a latent course and be overlooked. As a rule defense retains the upper hand in it; in any case alterations of the ego, comparable to scars, are left behind" (Freud 1939, p. 77).

28. In this context Fonagy (2001) refers to a fundamental difference in the image of humanity of the theory of attachment on the one hand and Freudian–Kleinian psychoanalysis on the other. According to Fonagy, Freud and Klein adhere to a tragic view of humankind in which conflict is at the center, whereas Bowlby defends a romantic and optimistic view of the development of humanity. By the latter, Fonagy means that according to Bowlby, development must principally be thought of as a process in which the possibilities of the child can progressively unfold. This development can only be disturbed by external factors. Pathology is an

Temporality in the Work of Freud and Bowlby

Bowlby's critique that Freud reconstructs childhood on the basis of analyses of adults instead of observing children scientifically must also be tempered in light of Freud's minimalistic concept of infantile sexuality. The infantile factor that will play a decisive role in puberty is an innocent experience of pleasure or a banal occurrence in childhood that only receives psychic significance and a truly instinctual character with the awakening of sexuality in puberty. Freud's notion of deferred action goes radically against the idea of normal development. This deferred action after all means that "experiences, impressions and memory-traces may be revised at a later date to fit in with fresh experiences or with the attainment of a new stage of development. They may in that event be endowed *not only with a new meaning but also with psychical effectiveness*" (Laplanche and Pontalis 1967, p. 111, italics added). The temporality of the psyche, in other words, is not linear. From Dora's case it becomes apparent what this means. The oral pleasure of thumb-sucking only receives psychic significance when it is afterward taken up and reworked into a phantasy of fellatio. Infantile sexuality also only receives its instinctual character afterward, when the lost experience of pleasure from childhood is once again targeted during adult sexuality. The phantasy of fellatio invokes the objectless, egoless, autoerotic pleasure of the first years of life, which has been lost to consciousness. For psychoanalysis, the direct observation of these first years of life consequently has only a secondary significance. Which experiences and impressions from early childhood will afterward be taken up in the sexual phantasies of the adult can after all as a matter of principle only be determined retrospectively (Green 2000).

---

unfortunate accident that could have been avoided. In Freud and Klein, on the contrary, the development is always and principally disturbed by the conflict between potentially pathological tendencies and the reaction formations that are an answer to them. As a consequence, no one completely escapes from pathology. This conflict, and the impossibility of providing a definitive and ultimate answer to it, determine the tragedy of human existence.

Klein, the Child, and the Psychotic Anxieties of the Baby

To understand the neurotic symptoms of his adult patients, Freud postulates an infantile factor that retroactively returns in adult sexuality.[29] In contrast to Freud, who did not analyze children, Klein mainly worked with children from the third or fourth year of their life onward. Could Klein not simply observe the children of whom Freud had to reconstruct the inclinations for any and all perversions, such that there would be no talk of deferred action? Could Klein not simply observe directly that which Freud had to deduce about childhood from the analysis of adults in order to elucidate adult pathology? And yet, Klein's analyses of children have nothing to do with the observation of children, any more than the analyses of adults can be considered psychological observations. The analyst listens. He doesn't observe. To what then did Klein listen? We have already pointed out that Klein too is looking for an archaic factor that is reactivated by the current situation. According to Klein, the archaic "psychotic" anxieties of the first months of life repeat themselves in the phobias and the symptoms of obsessional neuroses of her little patients. Unlike Freud, Klein interprets these archaic factors not in terms of erotic experiences of pleasure but as psychical mechanisms of defense.[30] When Richard, a 10-year-old boy who suffers from a social phobia, discusses his fear of Hitler, Klein presupposes that Richard is dealing with current anxieties that are linked to his father, his mother, and his brother, according to the same mechanisms with which he responded to the most primitive anxieties of helplessness and his own aggression in the first

---

29. "This postulated constitution, containing the germs of all the perversions, will only be demonstrable in children, even though in them it is only with modest degrees of intensity that any of the instincts can emerge. A formula begins to take shape which lays it down that the sexuality of neurotics has remained in, or been brought back to, an infantile state. Thus our interest turns to the sexual life of children, and we will now proceed to trace the play of influences which govern the evolution of infantile sexuality till its outcome in perversion, neurosis or normal sexual life" (Freud 1905b, p. 172).

30. One may recall what we have said previously: Kleinians interpret on the level of defense mechanisms rather than on the level of the contents of the free associations that are put forward by the patient.

months of his life. These conflicts, for instance that Richard must detach himself from (the proximity of) his mother in order to go to school, reactivate the paranoid-schizoid and the depressive positions toward the loss of the object during the first weeks and months of his existence. Richard's current problematic is then determined by the way in which he lived through the paranoid-schizoid and depressive positions as an infant. Klein (1961) understands Richard's fear of Hitler as projections of his own aggression and hence according to the model of paranoia.

In the associations of children, Klein discovers the deferred action of mechanisms of defense that dominated the life of the baby. This idea of a reactivation of archaic mechanisms differs essentially from Bowlby's model. According to Bowlby, the normal anxieties of a particular phase of life are overcome during the course of normal development. Only persons who in those phases of life are inadequately supported by their environment will develop pathologies later, because they have learned as children that they cannot count on a secure attachment (Bowlby 1973). Hence for Bowlby it would be absurd to link the normal anxieties of the baby, such as Klein does, with psychiatric syndromes. Paranoid schizophrenia and manic-depressive psychosis in adults, according to Klein, are merely magnifications and reactivations of the normal anxieties of the baby. Yet also in the affective experience of normal adult life, for example in the fear of loneliness, in love and jealousy, the same psychotic mechanisms are at work. Hence Klein understands normality, in children as well as adults, from the perspective of pathological structures that themselves go back to all of our earliest infancies. Just as Freud considers normal sexuality as a middle position between neurosis and perversion, Klein understands anxiety and guilt on the basis of their pathological forms in melancholia and paranoia.

Discussion

Freudian–Kleinian psychoanalysis is a clinical anthropology. In the analysis of pathological structures, Freud and Klein identify an infantile factor that in a more or less visible way is also at work in normal life. This means that pathologies are magnifications of tendencies that also dominate normal psychic functioning and that the difference between normality and pathology can only be one of degree. This insight is hardly reconcilable with Bowlby's—frankly, sophisticated—model of trauma, and with his theory of a pathogenesis in which normality and pathology must be thought of as strictly separate. Furthermore, Freud and Klein's psychoanalytic model implies a theory of temporality that can simply not be made to coincide with Bowlby's linear concept of time. However, this does not detract from the fact that Bowlby points to an essential dimension of human existence to which Freud and Klein do not do justice. The problematic of attachment cannot be understood adequately in Freud's dualistic theory of the instinct or on the basis of Klein's insights about the death instinct and anxiety.

Therefore, we must ask in which way the problematic of attachment can from the perspective of a clinical anthropology be conceived as an original dimension in the life of the instinct. How can we do justice to Bowlby's critique of Freud and Klein without abandoning the perspective of clinical anthropology? In his article "*Sich Anklammern— Auf Suche gehen*," Imre Hermann (1936) develops a proto-theory of attachment that not only conceives the problematic of attachment from the perspective of a clinical anthropology but also offers an interesting alternative to the death instinct in Freud and Klein. Consequently, we have every reason to subject this theory to a closer investigation.

IMRE HERMANN: A CLINICAL ANTHROPOLOGY OF ATTACHMENT?

Even among psychoanalysts, Hermann (1889–1984) is relatively unknown. Nevertheless, he is one of the more important representatives of the Hungarian school of psychoanalysis. His work has had a great influence on the thought of Balint, Bowlby, and Szondi, but only the latter recognized Hermann's originality. Hermann (1936) introduces a new dualism of instincts, explicitly as an alternative to the Freudian opposition between Eros and the death instinct. First we shall investigate which clinical problems encouraged Hermann to develop his own model of instincts. Then we shall investigate in which way he projects a clinical anthropology on the basis of this new theory of the instinct and to which extent this theory of attachment offers an alternative to the death instinct. In other words, Hermann succeeds in integrating the problematic of attachment into the Freudian–Kleinian perspective. At the same time, it becomes possible to continue the demystification of the concept of the death instinct that we started to undertake in our reading of Freud and Klein. This means that Hermann permits a reconciliation of the primacy of the child and of trauma with the problematic of attachment.

Clinging—Searching

To introduce the problem of attachment to psychoanalysis, Hermann relies on a few passages from Freud's *Three Essays on the Theory of Sexuality* and on a number of ethological studies of chimpanzees. Freud (1905b) concludes his discussion of the oral instinct and of thumb-sucking as follows: "In this connection a grasping-instinct may appear and may manifest itself as a simultaneous rhythmic tugging at the lobes or the ears or a catching hold of some part of another person (as a rule the ear) for the same purpose" (p. 180). After this remark in passing, the reference to the hand and grasping disappears from Freud's work. For Hermann, on the contrary, Freud's remark gives rise to explore the grasping instinct in a number of ethological studies of apes. In the behavior of these apes the instinct to grasp is much more clearly present than in the young child. In the first instance the instinct to grasp serves the purpose of clinging to the mother. Bowlby later also pointed out that this primitive form of attachment behavior is much more expressly present in apes than in humans (Bowlby 1969). Hermann as well as Bowlby remark that after some time another behavior comes to the fore: the child or young ape begins to explore the surrounding area, going out to investigate, while at the same time remaining apprehensive not to lose the contact with the mother. A back-and-forth between clinging (*sich anklammern*) to the mother and going out to search and explore (*auf die Suche gehen*) emerges.

In contrast to Bowlby, Hermann does not seek to investigate the normal development of attachment. His ethological interests are based solely on clinical and technical problems of psychoanalytic practice. First there are a number of pathologies that received little attention from Freud: dysthymic and depressive disturbances, erotomania, toxicomania, the compulsion to wander, and in general, all those pathologies in which the craving for ever new objects, or the nostalgia for the old, lost, and irreplaceable object, play the key role. Hermann (1936) refers to a patient with nymphomania: "She must find someone to whom she can cling. Especially in the case of unsatisfied sexual desires she is in such a state of tension that she has to pace back and forth in the room. She feels an urge to leave, *so as to cling to someone else*" (Hermann 1936, p. 358; translation by the authors; italics added). Hermann also refers to an analysand whose compulsive wandering usually ended with a visit to a prostitute. He then did not have any sexual contact with her, but simply paid her and went back home. Certain anxieties also fit into this dynamic of clinging and exploring: the fear of being abandoned and of losing one's hold on reality, the fear that one will be "dropped."

It is probable that another, technical, problematic also induced Hermann to study attachment. It is a well-known phenomenon that for many patients the setting of psychoanalytic treatment offers too uneasy a footing, grip, or "holding."[31] Just as Freud never explicitly thematized the problematic of attachment, he also never pointed out this technical difficulty in his writings on psychoanalytic technique. The ethological studies about the way in which young apes cling to their mothers provide Hermann with a model to think about this difficulty. Before the analysand can start to search for the meaning of his symptoms, the opposite tendency to cling to something must also have been met to some extent. Usually eye contact is sufficient to accomplish this, but the experiments of Ferenczi and Winnicott have shown that this eye contact is merely a sublimated form of literally clinging to the analyst (Ferenczi 1985, Little 2002). But also, analysts who do not literally hold the anxieties of their patients in their hands will be familiar with analysands who are only able

---

31. The classic setting entails that the analysand lie on a couch in a position in which she cannot see the analyst who sits behind her.

to speak if they can be assured that they are on a sufficiently steady footing. From this it emerges that the hands and eyes are first organs of clinging before they become the erogenous sources of sadism and voyeurism.

Hermann refers to a number of screen memories and dreams in which the themes of clinging and searching are prominent. The only thing that one of his patients is able to remember of a dream is "I am going. . . ." This patient sometimes has the tendency to walk around aimlessly. Another patient remembers that as a small child he could only fall asleep if he held onto something. Hermann then poses the question of whether these dreams and screen memories are secondary processes that must be analyzed further, or whether they are the expressions of an original instinctual impulse. The ethological studies of apes convince him that we must here be dealing with an original expression of the instinct.

Again, unlike Bowlby, Hermann is not interested in the further development of the attachment behavior. He does, however, ask a different question. If he encounters the tendencies of clinging and searching in the dreams, symptoms, and compulsive actions of his patients, this must mean that they are repressed or suppressed. Compulsion implies repression. Bowlby is right in saying that the primitive attachment behavior is overcome in the course of development and in a subsequent phase of development naturally makes room for a new form of attachment. However, as such this says nothing about the vicissitudes of these expressions of the instinct in the history of the subject. An example from the sexual sphere may clarify the distinction between natural development and subjective history. Like apes, the human being is by nature not very much interested in entering into sexual relations with other humans that he has grown up with. But this does not mean that the cultural incest taboo does not have a subjective effect. Even though cultural taboos to some extent always lean upon natural tendencies, their psychic effects are of a completely different order. The incest taboo turns family members into prohibited sexual partners. In this manner incest yet becomes an object of disgust, guilt, and fear, even though the prohibition of incest is inscribed in human nature.[32] The same

---

32. For the distinction between the incest taboo and a natural disgust of incest, see Van Coillie 2004.

obtains in the sphere of attachment. The tendency to cling to the mother by nature disappears in apes and children. Yet, for example, when parents at a certain moment consider their child big enough to forbid it to cling, and talk to it about it, this produces a cultural suppression of the instinct that must be distinguished from a natural overcoming of the instinct in a later stage of development. How are we to understand this?

According to Hermann, children are separated from their mother prematurely. The vicissitudes of early childhood attachment inevitably contain a series of traumatic and painful experiences of being abandoned. But only when the separation from the mother is symbolically marked by the adults—for example, by explicitly obliging the child to separate—can the child respond to this traumatic experience in a way that is not merely passive. Separation from the mother is no longer a fate, but has become a cultural task for the child. Because children can identify with the words of the adults, they want to be grown up and are able to distance themselves from the childish habit of clinging to the mother. The tendency to cling to the mother then becomes a source of shame. Big boys and girls do not cling to their mothers' apron-strings. The cultural suppression of the *Anklammerungstrieb* excludes and removes attachment from its natural development.[33] A psychic conflict between the urge to cling to the mother and the reactive tendency to be free of her emerges.[34] According to Hermann (1936), these conflicting tendencies support two contrary, phantasmatic representations: the phantasy of the lost unity with the mother, and the phantasy of total independence. These phantasmatic representations, which arose as a reaction to the cultural demand for detachment, repeat the archaic trau-

---

33. Hermann refers to this cultural and symbolic dimension by pointing to the primal father: "The conclusion offers itself, that the human child is—relative to the propensities of the instinct—prematurely torn from the body of the mother, perhaps even as a consequence of an egoistic deed of the primal father. *For this reason* the urge to cling continues to exist" (Hermann 1936, p. 351, italics added; see also Hermann 1941).

34. "In a first attempt we conceive of this separation, this tearing oneself away, as a reactive behavior such as, for example, cleanliness is to be understood as a reaction formation against anal erotism" (Hermann 1936, p. 363).

mas of attachment. The instinct to cling is now disappointed in relation to a phantasmatic dream of unity.

In this manner Hermann constructs two primal instincts: (1) clinging and searching; and (2) a reaction formation, the tendency to detach oneself from the primal object. Because of the fact that in the later manifestations of these instincts the infantile traumas of being abandoned repeat themselves, this complex of instincts takes on a compulsive and demonic character (Freud 1920). In relation to the phantasy of a pretraumatic unity with the mother, the instinct to cling is indeed inevitably frustrated. No real object can restore the phantasmatic unity with the mother. As a consequence attachment in humans is immersed in a sphere of nostalgia and inconsolability. The instinct to cling inevitably remains unsatisfied because any real object will merely be ersatz, an insufficient substitute for the phantasmatic primal object.

According to Hermann, this also explains the extraordinary aggression that characterizes humans, compared with other animals. The instinct of mastery, Hermann says, is not a primary instinct. It only emerges because of the frustration of the *Anklammerungstrieb*. Aggression is a form of clinging reinforced by frustration. Hermann (1936) writes: "I think I am able unmitigatedly to deduce the instinct of mastery in its aggressive form from the excessive tension and regressive cathexis of clinging. The attitude 'And if you are not willing, I will use force' is never so appropriate as in the instinct to cling" (Hermann 1936, p. 365; translated by the authors). Any human relationship in which the dream of unity may be sought is therefore also linked in essence with the risk of violence and aggression (Hermann 1941). According to Hermann, violence is based on the impossibility of relinquishing the dream of unity. Aggression is a form of nostalgia and a disavowal of inconsolability.

The instinct to explore likewise receives a compulsive character through the phantasy of the lost unity with the mother. Bowlby points out that exploring is a natural component of attachment behavior. But this cannot explain the compulsive character of searching and of human curiosity. In pathological as well as in sublimated forms of the instinct to search, it is apparent that this instinct exceeds the pleasure principle. The restless searching of someone who suffers from restlessness, and of the nymphomaniac, but also that of the scientist and the explorer, goes beyond what is still pleasurable. The compulsion to repeat shows that the ever new is taken up into a dynamic that circles the phantasy of the original and the unique, which has been lost.

We have already mentioned that the instinct to cling as a reaction formation evokes the tendency to detach and separate from the object.[35] Hermann (1936) compares this separation instinct with the obsession for order and cleanliness as a reaction to anal erotism. This separation instinct is at the same time an active repetition of the earlier traumatic separations that the child underwent passively. In the tendency to separate from the mother these traumatic separations are repeated in an intentional, and consequently nontraumatic, fashion (Freud 1926, Hermann 1936).

A typical example is the *Fort-Da* game of Freud's grandson, which we discussed in Chapter 1. The child, originally overwhelmed by the disappearance of the mother, repeats the traumatic experience actively by throwing the bobbin away, again and again. In Hermann's model we may understand this behavior as follows: (1) as a reaction formation against the frustrated wish to cling to the mother; and (2) as an intentional, and therefore nontraumatic, repetition of the separation from the mother. According to Hermann this is also the mechanism that underlies automutilation. The unbearable pain of the original trauma is repeated consciously, intentionally, and in measured doses. True, this too causes pain, but it is accompanied by a "narcissistic high" of total autonomy and detachment (Hermann 1936, p. 368). The psychic state that accompanies suicide attempts may perhaps also be described as a similar flush of absolute detachment and of a triumph over the (primal) object. These masochistic or self-destructive phenomena are, according to Hermann, the extreme forms of the reactive tendency to separate from the mother and of a tendency to overcome the archaic traumas of attachment by repeating them— one more time and now for good. In this sense these self-destructive

---

35. A reaction formation is the "psychological attitude or habitus diametrically opposed to a repressed wish, and constituted as a reaction against it (e.g., bashfulness countering exhibitionistic tendencies). In economic terms, reaction formation is the counter-cathexis of a conscious element; equal in strength to the unconscious cathexis, it works in the contrary direction" (Laplanche and Pontalis 1967, p. 376).

phenomena are also attempts at a cure and recovery, attempts to let the separation occur for once in a good and controlled fashion.[36]

An Alternative to the Death Instinct?

Hermann (1936) explicitly presents his model of attachment as an alternative to certain aspects of the Freudian and Kleinian death instinct. Freud introduced the death instinct in order to clarify a number of clinical phenomena: the compulsive repetition of traumatic events, the extraordinary power of aggressive and destructive tendencies in human beings, and the mysterious masochism in human sexuality and in our relation to morality. In Melanie Klein's work, the death instinct mainly plays a part in the analysis of aggression and guilt feelings. The death instinct, then, serves to explain the obsessive and demonic aspects of human nature. We have called the existence of such a term, biologically speaking, improbable, and redundant in reference to clinical practice. Freud's idea that aggression is a tendency toward self-destruction that has shifted onto the external world, does not provide a better insight into the origin of that aggression. It remains equally unclear how Freud perceives the link between aggression and the death instinct when the death instinct is at the same time identified to a desire for nirvana. Furthermore, nowhere in his clinical studies after 1920 does Freud address the death instinct in any great detail, but instead emphasizes infantile helplessness and the influence of early childhood trauma much more than he had before (Freud 1926, 1927, 1937, 1939, 1940b). Helplessness and trauma appear to be the clinical counterpart to metapsychological speculation about the death instinct (see Chapter 1).

Freud and Klein think of this helplessness in terms of the basic experiences of hunger and thirst.[37] They see attachment merely as a

---

36. The desire to leave on "good" terms may also play an important role in the final stages of therapy.

37. Laplanche and Pontalis (1967) define Freudian helplessness as follows: "The state of the human suckling, which being entirely dependent on other people for the satisfaction of their needs (hunger, thirst), proves incapable of carrying out the specific action necessary to put an end to the internal tension" (p. 189).

remedy for this helplessness. Hermann raises the objection that the bond with the mother cannot be considered a mere emergency measure. The need to be in the vicinity of the mother occurs in all higher primates as an original innate tendency. No one escapes from being left on one's own once in a while, just as everyone will sooner or later be obliged to separate from his or her mother. This is one of the inevitable vicissitudes of attachment. For this reason Hermann postulates a universal experience of insecurity (*Haltlosigkeit*—lack of a hold, having nothing to hold on to).[38] The loss of the object is not primarily a problem of the vital needs of hunger and thirst; it is first and foremost a loss of ground. According to Hermann, the most basic anxiety is consequently not the fear of the tension of needs (Freud) or the fear of the death instinct, but the fear of being abandoned by others. The primal catastrophe according to Hermann is not a question of hunger, but the traumatic separation from the mother to whom we cling, and who holds us tight. From the perspective of this *Haltlosigkeit*, Hermann proceeds to give a concrete analysis of the phenomena that Freud and Klein consider to be manifestations of the death instinct.

Hermann's analysis of aggression as a form of clinging that is characterized by frustration provides a much more concrete idea of the origin of aggression than Freud's concept of a death instinct that has been projected outward. The link between aggression and nirvana, which remains somewhat mysterious in Freud, becomes much easier to imagine concretely in Hermann's model. Aggression, according to Hermann, is after all only the reaction to the frustration of the dream of unity with the primal object.

According to Freud and Klein, self-destructive tendencies are the most original manifestations of the death instinct. The death instinct aims at the self-destruction of the organism. Hermann's analysis of automutilation, the compulsion to repeat, and masochism as attempts to separate from the mother provides the first clinically useful model for an analysis of these phenomena. They are reaction formations against the frustrated desire to cling to the primal object, just as the compulsion to cleanliness and order is a reaction formation to anal erotism.

---

38. *Haltlos*, without foothold or basis, uncontrolled, *Haltlosigkeit*: inconsistent, weak, lack of foothold, groundlessness, without any grasp on anything.

Hermann's theory of the instinct also provides concrete support for Klein's theory of paranoid-schizoid and depressive positions (Hermann 1941). Klein understands these positions as reactions of the early ego to its own aggression toward the object. Hermann demonstrates that this aggression itself may be seen as a form of nostalgia and inconsolability. Klein's damaged object, which turns against the self or which must be repaired by it, originally was also the object to which the child wanted to cling. The loss of the object is then also in the first instance a loss of stable ground. It is this *Haltlosigkeit* of the subject that gives rise to aggression and the feelings of guilt that ensue. *Haltlosigkeit* rather than the vital *Hilflosigkeit* lies at the basis of the phenomena that Freud and Klein consider manifestations of the death instinct.

CONCLUSION: A CLINICAL ANTHROPOLOGY OF ATTACHMENT

With clinging, searching, and the separation from the object, Hermann describes three dimensions that coincide with the various forms of attachment behavior such as Bowlby was to investigate much later on. From the ethological studies of apes, Hermann, too, concludes that these dimensions are original expressions of the instinct, and hence need not be reduced to the sexual instinct or the instinct of self-preservation. But while Bowlby strongly maintains a strict distinction between pathology and normality,[39] Hermann's theory of the instinct is a clinical anthropology. The extreme pathological phenomena described by Hermann are based on the same psychic mechanisms as the normal forms of attachment and detachment/separation. After all, like those normal manifestations, these phenomena refer back to one universal catastrophe: infantile *Haltlosigkeit*. The reactions of the child to that experience—

---

39. On the relation between normality and pathology in psychoanalysis and the theory of attachment, Fonagy (2001) writes: "The psychoanalytic perspective might encourage us to think less categorically and more dimensionally about attachment security. The potential for both security and insecurity is likely to be present in all of us" (p. 187).

reactions that in childhood are still variable and flexible—during the course of childhood, and in particular during puberty, crystallize to form a specific mixture of nostalgia, aggressivity, attempts at separation, and a tendency to explore. This attachment behavior, however, is never anything else than an attempt to learn to deal with the experience of being without a foothold, grip, or basis.

These vicissitudes of attachment in the history of the subject must not be confused with the natural phases of development of attachment such as have been described by Bowlby, for example. Through the premature separation from the mother, by a cultural demand, attachment behavior is withdrawn from its natural course in human beings. The *Haltlosigkeit* and inconsolability that are the fate of human beings, arise as a reaction to the cultural demand of separation from the original object and hence are an important part of civilization and its discontents. This discontent differs only by degree from the pathological forms of detachment and inconsolability. "Quantitative disharmonies must be held responsible for the suffering of the neurotic" (Freud 1940, p. 183). According to Freud, this insight is "one of our most important results."

4

Attachment, Aggression, and Sexuality

DEATH INSTINCT, *HILFLOSIGKEIT*, AND *HALTLOSIGKEIT*

In *Beyond the Pleasure Principle*, Freud (1920) had introduced the death instinct in order to elucidate a number of clinical problems. The compulsion to repeat in traumatic neurosis, and in particular posttraumatic dreams, cannot be explained from the perspective of Freud's first theory of the instinct. After all, this theory implies that all psychic activity aims at the attainment of pleasure or the avoidance of unpleasure, which simply does not work in the cases of the compulsion to repeat and posttraumatic dreams. The death instinct points to a demonic dynamic in human instinctual life. The instinct is ultimately not directed toward satisfaction, but toward the return to the inorganic and a complete extinction of desire. The reference to the death instinct, however, remains extremely general and abstract in Freud's work. It is probably not a coincidence that Freud hardly mentions the death instinct in his clinical work. However, this does not mean that the introduction of the death instinct did not have any influence on clinical practice. After 1920, Freud emphasizes more than previously the importance of negative experiences, of infantile traumas and of the radical helplessness of the young child. This emphasis on the helplessness of the young child then also appears to be the clinical translation of Freud's metapsychological innovations in *Beyond the Pleasure Principle*. With regard to clinical practice, Freud appears to be in agreement with Ferenczi's complaint that the death instinct expressed an activity, while the traumatic experiences and helplessness of early childhood are a matter of radical passivity.[1] The idea of a biological

---

1. In connection with trauma and *Hilflosigkeit*, Ferenczi (1985) writes in his *Journal Clinique*: "Every thing that lives probably reacts to its dissolution beginning with its fragmentation (death instinct?). But instead of 'death instinct,' one will instead have to choose a word which expresses the complete passivity of this process" (p. 270).

instinct of self-destruction is then superfluous and confusing. It adds nothing to the idea of an infantile helplessness that later in life repeats itself as a trauma to which the subject cannot but relate in order to resist its own decline into radical passivity.

Freud is only able to think of the traumatic helplessness at the origin of human subjectivity in very basic terms of hunger and thirst. These needs give rise to traumatic experiences because they are essentially dependent on the outside world for their satisfaction. Indeed, Freud considers all other instincts, including aggression and curiosity, to be sexual instincts. This means that they only aim at pleasure regardless of their object, and that they are originally satisfied in and on one's own body. Sexual instincts can then not be vulnerable to trauma in the same way that vital needs are. They have no need of external objects and can also be satisfied in and by one's own body. In the absence of the mother, hunger cannot be sated, but oral sexuality finds the same satisfaction in thumb-sucking as in suckling. Initially sexuality is autoerotic and objectless. Only with regard to vital needs is the child in a position of radical helplessness and dependency. According to Freud, this dependency is the source for the child's attachment to the mother. The child seeks the proximity of the mother and fears her absence because it knows that without her it is delivered over to the horror of basic frustrations such as hunger and thirst.

Melanie Klein, too, sees attachment from the perspective of the satisfaction of needs. According to Klein, children are attacked by the death instinct from within and this death instinct is in the first instance directed against their own ego. The experiences of hunger and thirst give a first localization to the primitive anxiety of death, which was initially only experienced as an unlocalizable and nameless experience of corporeal destruction and psychological disintegration. Hunger localizes the death instinct in the oral zone and thereby immediately opens the possibility of evacuating the death instinct outside into the "bad" breast. The life instinct, in contrast, receives its first form in the "good" breast, which initially coincides with the corporeal experience of satisfaction. The later attachment to the mother is based on these experiences of satisfaction and frustration. Children seek the proximity of the mother because she is the source of the satisfaction of their needs and because they need to reassure themselves that she has survived the phantasmatic aggressive attacks with which they react to the experience of frustration. However, in her later texts, Klein suggests in a number of places that there must be an original innate understanding of a link with the mother that cannot be conceived of in terms of need and anxiety.

Already in 1936—and therefore long before the publication of the classical texts of Kleinian psychoanalysis—the Hungarian psychoanalyst Imre Hermann developed the idea that attachment to the mother could not be reduced to more basic interests or needs. The ethological studies of young chimpanzees show that from birth, they are directed toward the mother and cling to her. Hermann also identifies this tendency to cling in human babies. However, in humans this tendency is frustrated prematurely. The child is then inundated by a feeling of abandonment or, more precisely, the feeling of having nothing left to hold. This *Haltlosigkeit*, according to Hermann, must not be deduced from a basic *Hilflosigkeit* or the baby's knowledge that without the mother he is subject to hunger and thirst. The fear of this loss of ground is an original anxiety that provides the basis for aggressivity. Out of the anxiety that the mother will abandon the child, he clings to the mother with all his force. The frustration of this clinging transforms the clinging into an aggressive instinct of mastery. When the child is left alone, his empty hands clench into a fist. The clinging fingers turn into strangling claws. Behind this aggression we find a phantasmatic desire for the lost unity of mother and child. But the frustrations of clinging can also lead to the reaction formation of separating from the mother at all costs. This tendency to separation is not an original instinct but the effect of the cultural suppression of the instinctual tendency to cling to the mother. This active tendency to separation repeats in a nontraumatic manner the earlier separation from the mother that the child endured passively. Expressions of the instinct, which from the point of the observer would prove self-destructive or masochistic, are, according to Hermann, attempts to separate oneself from the mother and to deal with the earlier traumatic separation.

The self-destructive and aggressive tendencies that led Freud and Klein to turn the death instinct into a central notion of their psychoanalytic theory may be analyzed using Hermann's model of attachment in a more concrete and insightful manner than with Freud and Klein, in whose theories the death instinct remains a cosmological or biological myth, the clinical relevance of which can hardly be demonstrated.

From Lost Object to Damaged Object

According to Melanie Klein, the paranoid-schizoid and the depressive position are two fundamental psychic constellations that determine the subject's relation toward its own aggression. In the paranoid-schizoid position, the subject projects or evacuates its aggression onto the object. The anxiety that characterizes this position is the anxiety that the object avenge this aggression. "An eye for an eye, a tooth for a tooth" is the only valid law. The paranoid-schizoid position is dominated by the anxiety of being persecuted and destroyed by the vengeful object damaged by my aggression. In the depressive position the subject comes to the painful realization that the hated object is also the love object. The depressive position is then characterized by feelings of guilt and the need to repair the damage caused. When the subject despairs of its capacities to repair the damaged object, the paranoid-schizoid anxiety that the object will take revenge for irreparable damage caused by the aggression of the subject upon the object threatens anew.

According to Klein, the aggression against the external world is a redirection of the death instinct that in the first instance aims at self-destruction. Klein's metapsychology is then not an object-relation theory or theory of attachment. It is not of itself that the instinct is aimed at an object. The object functions in the first instance as a container in which we can dump our aggression, which properly speaking is self-destructive. Klein's object is like a punching bag that takes my place, on which I can abreact my own aggression directed against myself. The question remains how we can reconcile this concept of the function of the object with Klein's suggestion that the bond with the mother is instinctive and innate. Hermann's notion that aggression arises out of the frustration of the instinctual tendency to cling offers in our view a more insightful and clinically more useful analysis of aggression. It allows us to analyze the transference further than Klein's idea that attachment to the object is merely an attempt to save oneself from self-destruction. Hermann's analysis of aggression further does not detract from Klein's ingenious discovery of the depressive and paranoid-schizoid positions as attitudes taken by subjects toward their own aggression.[2]

However, the insight that the link with the mother is original and cannot be reduced to experiences of the satisfaction of needs does cast doubt on Klein's description of infantile phantasies in terms of a primary orality. If, as Bowlby and Hermann have shown, love does not go through the stomach, Klein's exclusive metaphorical language of the breast, of milk, and of love no longer works. In Freud as well as in Hermann, the organs of the instinct of mastery and of aggression are the hands and more generally the muscles. But Klein's construction of the primitive aggression of the child always deals with oral aggression. This means that according to Klein's theory aggression and the instinct of mastery always are anaclitically dependent on the oral experience of pleasure. Behind oral aggression, which is itself anaclitically related to the oral experience of pleasure and the experience of hunger and thirst, Klein presupposes a pure instinct of destruction. In Klein's anaclitic theory of aggression, the death instinct kidnaps the libido.[3]

According to Hermann, aggression is not a primitive fact that cannot be analyzed further. Aggression or the death instinct are not the end terms of analysis. According to Hermann, aggression is not a projection of the death instinct but a frustrated form of wishing to cling to the object. It is only through the frustration of this instinct to cling that the tendency to master the object in an aggressive fashion is

---

2. This is in contrast to the thought that preceding the paranoid-schizoid position we must presuppose another position or phase in which no clear distinctions are yet given and in which the child is supposed to exist in a sort of undifferentiated harmony with reality (Dehing 1998). From the perspective of the Kleinian doctrine of the instinct, this idea is incoherent. We are dealing here with a phantasy—and therefore not a new position—the clinical relevance of which has been demonstrated by Hermann.

3. In contrast to Freud, Klein does not really address the question of whether oral libido may be called sexual in the strict sense of the term. That in Kleinian psychoanalysis the libido is taken to be an alibi for pure destruction demonstrates that two world wars separate the *Three Essays on the Theory of Sexuality* and Klein's later works.

evoked. Aggression may be analyzed as the impossibility of relinquishing the phantasmatic unity with the primal object. The clinical importance of this insight, which would be obscured by the reference to a death instinct, can hardly be overestimated.

The Oedipus Complex: From Lost Object to Forbidden Object

The affirmation of the primacy of the child and of trauma forces us to reformulate the place and the significance of sexuality. We have pointed out that in the later texts by Freud and Klein, sexuality's function is to "bind" a more primitive trauma. Freud here emphasizes anal erotism and castration. In extension thereof, Klein and Hermann emphasize oedipal sexuality. Freud understands the Oedipus complex primarily from the perspective of the development of the sexual instinct. In view of the fact that with Klein as well as with Hermann the central psychoanalytic problematic is not infantile sexuality but loss of the object or separation from the mother, the oedipal complex, too, primarily must be understood from the perspective of the loss of the object. It is a way to deal with that trauma. What does this mean?

First and foremost, the mother is the lost object. Klein understands the Oedipus complex from the perspective of the loss of the object,[4] and there are reasons for this. After all, to enter into the Oedipus complex means that the absence of the object that satisfies vital needs is from now on understood in light of a rivalry with another object.[5] In the oedipal scheme, the mother, according to Hermann, is transformed from an object of attachment to a sex object and therefore from a lost object to a forbidden object. After all, in the course of childhood the incest barrier develops (Freud 1905a). At the same time, the aggression that arises on the basis of the experience of the loss of the object is transformed into rivalry with a third. In this way the

---

4. For Klein this object, however, is, as we well know, not an object of attachment but primarily an object that satisfies our vital needs.

5. See Chapter 2. On the idea of the Oedipus complex as a transformation of a more fundamental problematic, see Van Haute and Geyskens 2004.

Oedipus complex offers a restructuring of the original *Haltlosigkeit* and of aggression.

In *Constructions in Analysis*, Freud (1937) claims that the task of the analyst consists in reconstructing the analysand's traumatic experiences from earliest childhood. In this context Freud emphasizes that these constructions do not aim at objective knowledge of the past. Whether these constructions contain a kernel of truth is seen much more clearly from the fact that they may evoke new memories and further associations in the analysand. Constructions are always incomplete, cursory, and ultimately only specific for this particular analysand and this particular analyst. And yet, one may discover a few universal characteristics. The experiences of early childhood, which, according to Freud, return in neurotic symptoms and psychotic delusions, have always been forgotten, are always traumatic, and always have a destructive or sexual content (Freud 1939). Following in Freud's, Klein's, and Hermann's footsteps, we have attempted to subject these general characteristics to a closer investigation. Our interpretation of attachment, aggression, and sexuality in Freud, Klein, and Hermann can then also be no more than a metaconstruction that is general but not universal. Psychoanalytic theory is essentially incomplete and precursory. It waits, in expectation of the next analysand.

References

Balint, A. (1937). Love for the mother and mother love. In *Primary Love and Psychoanalytic Technique*, ed. M. Balint, pp. 109–127. London: Karnac/Maresfield Library, 1994.

Balint, M. (1937). Early developmental states of the ego: primary object-love. In *Primary Love and Psychoanalytic Technique*, ed. M. Balint, pp. 90–108. London: Karnac/Maresfield Library, 1994.

———— (1952). New beginning and the paranoid and depressive syndromes. In *Primary Love and Psychoanalytic Technique*, ed. M. Balint, p. 244–265. London: Karnac/Maresfield Library, 1994.

Bion, W. (1962). *Learning from Experience*. London: Karnac.

Bowlby, J. (1958). The nature of the child's tie to his mother. In *International Journal of Psycho-Analysis* 39:350–373.

———— (1969). *Attachment and Loss, vol. 1: Attachment*. New York: Basic Books.

———— (1973). *Attachment and Loss, vol. 2: Separation, Anxiety, and Anger*. New York: Basic Books.

Declercq, F. (2000). *Het Reële bij Lacan*. Gent: Idesca.

Dehing, J. (1998). *Een Bundel Intense duisternis*. Antwerpen: Garant.

Dekesel, M. (2002). *Eros en Ethiek*. Leuven: Acco.

Dennett, D. C. (1995). *Darwin's Dangerous Idea*. London/New York: Penguin.

Ferenczi, S. (1916). Two types of war neuroses. In *Selected Writings*, pp. 129–144. London: Penguin, 1999.

——— (1934). *Réflections sur le traumatisme*. In *Oeuvres Complètes*, part IV, pp. 139–147. Paris: Editions Payot.

——— (1968–1985). *Oeuvres Complètes: 4 Parts Plus Journal Clinique*. Paris: Editions Payot.

——— (1985). *Journal Clinique* (Clinical Diary). Paris: Editions Payot.

Fonagy, P. (2001). *Attachment Theory and Psychoanalysis*. New York: Other Press.

Freud, A. (1914). On the theory of analysis of children. In *Heirs to Freud: Essays in Freudian Psychology*, ed. H. M. Ruitenbeek, 1966, p. 128–142. New York: Grove.

Freud, S. (1887–1904a). *The Complete Letters of Sigmund Freud to Wilhelm Fliess 1887–1904*, ed. and trans. J. M. Masson. Cambridge/London: Belknap Press of Harvard University Press, 1985.

——— (1887–1904b). *Briefe an Wilhelm Fliess 1887–1904*, ed. J. M. Masson. Frankfurt am Main: S. Fischer Verlag, 1986.

——— (1895). Entwurf einer wissenschaftlichen Psychologie. [Project for a scientific psychology.] In *Aus den Anfangen der Psychoanalyse. Briefe an Wilhelm Fliess, Abhandlungen und-Notizen aus Denahren 1887–1902*, ed. M. Bonaparte, A. Freud, and E. Kris, pp. 297–384. London: Imago, 1950; Frankfurt am Main: S. Fischer Verlag, 1962.

——— (1900). The interpretation of dreams. *Standard Edition* 4/5.

——— (1901). The psychopathology of everyday life. *Standard Edition* 6.

——— (1905a). Jokes and their relation to the unconscious. *Standard Edition* 8.

——— (1905b). Three essays on the theory of sexuality. *Standard Edition* 7:123–246.

——— (1905c). Fragment of an analysis of a case of hysteria. *Standard Edition* 7:7–122.

——— (1908a). Character and anal erotism. *Standard Edition* 9:167–175.

——— (1908b). On the sexual theories of children. *Standard Edition* 9:205–225.

——— (1909). Notes upon a case of obsessional neurosis. *Standard Edition* 10:153–318.

——— (1913a). The disposition to obsessional neurosis. *Standard Edition* 12:317–326.

——— (1913b). Preface to Bourke's *Scatological Rites of All Nations*. *Standard Edition* 12:333–337.

——— (1914a). Remembering, repeating, and working through. *Standard Edition* 12:145–156.

——— (1914b). On narcissism: an introduction. *Standard Edition* 14:67–104.

——— (1915a). Instincts and their vicissitudes. *Standard Edition* 14:109–140.

——— (1915b). The unconscious. *Standard Edition* 14:159–204.

——— (1917a). On the transformations of instincts, as exemplified in anal erotism. *Standard Edition* 17:125–133.

——— (1917b). Mourning and melancholia. *Standard Edition* 14:237–258.

——— (1919). A child is being beaten. *Standard Edition* 17:177–204.

——— (1920). Beyond the pleasure principle. *Standard Edition* 18:1–64.

——— (1923). The ego and the id. *Standard Edition* 19:1–66.

——— (1924). The economic problem of masochism. *Standard Edition* 19:159–170.

——— (1926). Inhibitions, symptoms, and anxiety. *Standard Edition* 19:71–76.

——— (1927). Fetishism. *Standard Edition* 21:152–157.

——— (1930). Civilization and its discontents. *Standard Edition* 21:57–146.

——— (1937). Constructions in analysis. *Standard Edition* 23:255–269.

——— (1939). Moses and monotheism. *Standard Edition* 23:1–138.

——— (1940a). An outline of psycho-analysis. *Standard Edition* 23:139–208.

——— (1940b). Splitting of the ego in the process of defense. *Standard Edition* 23:275–278.

Geyskens, T. (2003). Over de rol van de puberteit als biologische rots in Freud's metapsychologie. *Tijdschrift voor psychoanalyse* 1:17–26.

Green, A. (1990). *Le Complexe de Castration.* Paris: PUF.

——— (2000). *La Diachronie en Psychanalyse.* Paris: Minuit.

Heimann, P. (1952). Notes on the theory of the life and death instincts. In *Developments in Psycho-Analysis*, ed. M. Klein, P. Heimann, S. Isaacs, and J. Rivière. London: Hogarth.

——— (1955). A contribution to the re-evaluation of the Oedipus complex—the early stages. In *New Directions in Psychoanalysis*, ed. M. Klein, P. Heimann, and R. E. Money-Kyrle, pp. 23–38. London: Karnac, 1985.

Hermann, I. (1933). Zum Triebleben der Primaten. Bemerkurgen Zu S. Zuckerman: Social life of monkeys and apes. *Imago* 19:113–125.

——— (1936). Sich Anklammern—Auf Suche gehen. *International Zeitschrift für Psychoanalyse* 22:349–370.

——— (1941). Anklammerung, Feuer und Schamgefühl. *International Zeitschrift für Psychoanalyse und Imago* 26:252–274.

Hinshelwood, R. D. (1994). *Clinical Klein.* London: Free Association.

Isaacs, S. (1948). Nature and function of phantasy. *International Journal of Psycho-Analysis*, 29:73–97.

King, P., and Steiner, R., eds. (1991). *The Freud–Klein Controversies 1941–1945.* London: Institute of Psychoanalysis.

Klein, M. (1928). Early stages of the Oedipus conflict. In *Love, Guilt, and Reparation, and Other Works 1921–1945*, pp. 186–198. London: Virago, 1988.

———— (1930). The importance of symbol-formation in the development of the ego. In *Love, Guilt, and Reparation, and Other Works 1921–1945*, pp. 219–232. London: Virago, 1988.

———— (1932). *The Psychoanalysis of Children.* London: Vintage, 1997.

———— (1935). A contribution to the psychogenesis of manic-depressive states. In *Love, Guilt, and Reparation, and Other Works 1921–1945*, pp. 262–289. London: Virago, 1988.

———— (1937). Love, guilt, and reparation. In *Love, Guilt, and Reparation, and Other Works 1921–1945*, pp. 306–343. London: Virago, 1988.

———— (1940). Mourning and its relation to manic-depressive states. In *Love, Guilt, and Reparation, and Other Works 1921–1945*, pp. 344–369. London: Virago, 1988.

———— (1945). The Oedipus complex in the light of early anxieties. In *Love, Guilt, and Reparation, and Other Works 1921–1945*, pp. 370–419. London: Virago, 1988.

———— (1946). Notes on some schizoid mechanisms. In *Envy and Gratitude and Other Works*, pp. 1–24. New York: Free Press, 1984.

———— (1948). On the theory of anxiety and guilt. In *Envy and Gratitude and Other Works*, pp. 25–43. New York: Free Press, 1984.

———— (1952). Some theoretical conclusions regarding the emotional life of the infant. In *Envy and Gratitude and Other Works*, pp. 61–93. New York: Free Press, 1984.

———— (1957). Envy and gratitude. In *Envy and Gratitude and Other Works*, pp. 176–235. New York: Free Press, 1984.

———— (1959). Our adult world and its roots in infancy. In *Envy and Gratitude and Other Works*, pp. 247–263. New York: Free Press, 1984.

———— (1960). On mental health. In *Envy and Gratitude and Other Works*, pp. 268–274. New York: Free Press, 1984.

———— (1961). *Narrative of a Child Analysis.* London: Virago, 1988.

———— (1963). On the sense of loneliness. In *Envy and Gratitude and Other Works*, pp. 300–313. New York: Free Press, 1984.

———— (1984). *Envy and Gratitude and Other Works.* New York: Free Press.

Kristeva J. (1984). Julia Kristeva in conversation with Rosalind Coward. In *The Portable Kristeva*, ed. K. Oliver, pp. 331–348. New York: Columbia University Press, 1997.

Lacan, J., (1948). Aggressivity in psychoanalysis. In *Ecrits: A Selection*, pp. 9–32. New York: Routledge, 1977.

———— (1949). The mirror stage as formative of the function of the I. In *Ecrits: A Selection*, pp. 1–9. New York: Routledge, 1977.

———— (1975). *Les Écrits Techniques de Freud, le Séminaire de Jacques Lacan*, vol. 1, ed. J.-A. Miller. Paris: Seuil.

———— (1977). *Ecrits: A Selection*, trans. A. Sheridan. London/New York: Routledge.

Laplanche, J. (1992). Notes sur l'après-coup. In *Entre Séduction et Inspiration: l'Homme*, ed. J. Laplanche, pp. 57–66. Paris: PUF/Coll. Quadrige, 1999.

Laplanche, J., and Pontalis, J-B. (1967). *Vocabulaire de la Psychanalyse*. Paris: PUF. English trans.: *The Language of Psychoanalysis*, ed. D. N. Smith. London: Karnac, 1973.

Likierman, M. (2001). *Melanie Klein: Her Work in Context*. London/New York: Continuum.

Little, M. (2002). Lorsque Winnicott travaille dans des zones ou dominent les angoisses psychotiques—un compte-rendu personnel. In *Transfert et États Limites*, pp. 105–155. Paris: PUF.

McDougall, J. (1996). *Eros au Mille et un Visages*. Paris: Gallimard.

Meltzer, D. (1994). *The Kleinian Development*. Paris: Bayard.

Merleau-Ponty, M. (1945). *Phénoménologie de la Perception*. Paris: Gallimard. (English trans.: *Phenomenology of Perception*, trans. C. Smith. London: Routledge & Kegan, 1962.)

Moyaert, P. (1981).Taal, lichamelijkheid en affect in de schizofrenie I, II. *Tijdschrift voor psychiatrie* 24:49–69, 696–707.

Petot, J.-M. (1990). *Melanie Klein, vol. 1: First Discoveries and First System 1913–1932*. Madison, CT: International Universities Press.

Rivière, J. (1936). On the genesis of psychical conflict in early infancy. In *Developments in Psycho-Analysis*, ed. M. Klein, P. Heimann, S. Isaacs, and J. Rivière, pp. 37–66. London: Hogarth, 1952.

———— (1952). General introduction. In *Developments in Psycho-Analysis*, ed. M. Klein, P. Heimann, S. Isaacs, and J. Rivière. London: Hogarth.

Roustang, F. (2000). *Comment faire rire un paranoïaque*. Paris: Poches Odile Jacob.

Schokker, J., and Schokker, T. (2000). *Extimiteit. Jacques Lacans terugkeer naar Freud*. Meppel: Boom.

Schotte, J. (1990). *Szondi avec Freud. Sur la Voie d'une Psychiatrie Pulsionelle*. Brussels: Bibliothèque de patho-analyse, Editions Universitaires De Boeck.

Segal, H. (1964). *Introduction to the Work of Melanie Klein*. New York: Basic Books.

———— (1979). *Klein*. London: Fontana Galgow.

Stoller, R. (1968). *Sex and Gender. On the Development of Masculinity and Femininity*. London: Hogarth.

Van Coillie, F. (1998). Omtrent psychoanalyse en dood. *Tijdschrift voor Psychoanalyse* 2:70–85.

———— (1999). Het fantasma van de doodsdrift, *Tijdschrift voor Psychoanalyse* 3:137–153.

———— (2004). Zijn psychische stoornissen specifiek menselijk? Over het verschil tussen mens en dier. In *De Ongenode Gast. Zes psycho-Analytische Essays over het Verlangen en de Dood*, ed. F. Van Coillie, pp. 115–162. Amsterdam: Boom.

Van Haute, P. (2002). *Against Adaption. Jacques Lacan's Subversion of the Subject*. New York: Other Press.

———— (2005). Lacan leest Klein: over symbolisatie en de ontwikkeling van het ik. In *Mentalisaties*, ed. R. Vermote and R. Kinet, pp. 55–67. Leuven: Garant.

Van Haute, P., and Geyskens, T. (2004). *Confusion of Tongues: The Primacy of Sexuality in Freud, Ferenczi, and Laplanche*. New York: Other Press.

Winnicott, D. W. (1989). The psychology of madness: a contribution from psycho-analysis. In *Psychoanalytic Explorations*, ed. D. W. Winnicott, pp. 119–129. Cambridge, MA: Harvard University Press.

Index

affect
  in phantasies, 82, 84
  in repetition of trauma, xii
  reversal, 117–118
aggression/aggressivity, 60, 108, 138
  anxiety and, 45, 120–121
  benefits of learning to deal with, 90
  causes of, 23, 59–60, 90, 131, 140
  death instinct and, 38, 129
  in depressive position, 39
  fear of, 52n26, 74, 78, 120–121
  fearing damage to mother by, 86,
     109n13, 137
  frustration of clinging instinct
     and, 127, 130, 137–140
  objects of, 44–45, 51–52, 59–60,
     66–67, 69, 74, 138
  in paranoid-schizoid position, 71–
     72
  as sadism, 104–105

amnesia, infantile, 8–10
analysts, 124–125, 141
anger, 59
  about helplessness, 109–110
  aimless, 51–52
anxiety
  absence of, 42–43
  of death, 46–49, 136
  defenses against, 38–39
  in depressive position, 44n13, 61–
     63, 77–78
  of ego, 37, 48
  in evolutionary theory, xv, 112–113
  fundamental, 46–47
  infantile, 42, 46n16, 120
  in Klein's developmental phases,
     38–39
  in oral sadistic phase, 43
  in paranoid-schizoid position,
     44n13, 61, 64, 71–72, 75–78